Praise for this book:

I found this book amazing and couldn't put it down. I salute the author and his family for their dedication and service to these poor children and their mothers.
Enlisting and training uneducated mothers and making them the vehicle to teach others is almost unbelievable. However, it is happening, and that is what makes the story about this project so fascinating.

**– Wilfrid Wilkinson, Past President,
Rotary International**

Gem's book will make you laugh and cry at the same time. In your hands, you are holding a heart-rending account of a courageous family in the depths of the world's worst slums making changes that everyone said were impossible. If you want to be uplifted, read this book.

**– Michael Maloney,
best-selling author of Teach Your Children Well**

I believe that if you haven't walked the streets, you can't really understand. I have worked in the slums of Santo Domingo, but those experiences had not prepared me for what I read. I could go on for pages, but suffice to say that the world needs many, many more with the kind of commitment shown in this book, because that is how the world is going to change.

**– Douglas Crowe,
International Aid Consultant**

I thoroughly enjoyed this book. To teach one is our humane duty. To teach one to teach others is to achieve unasked for grace. Multiply that, as the Munro family has done, manna falls on Bangladesh. Read this book at bedsides, boardrooms and charitable brunches.

– Dirk McLean, best-selling author

*Best wishes
to Barbara*

G.E.M. Munro

*South Asian Adventures
with the
Active Poor*

Best wishes
to Barbara

C.C.M.M...

South Asian Adventures with the Active Poor

G.E.M. MUNRO

with sketches by the author

TAN*GENT* BOOKS, INC.

Cover photograph by Gabriel Munro.
Back cover photograph by G. M. Gray

Printed and bound in Canada.

Library and Archives Canada Cataloguing in Publication

ISBN 978-0-9688886-1-2

1. Munro, G. E. M. (George Edward Mitford), 1951- --Travel --Bangladesh--Dhaka. 2. Dhaka (Bangladesh)--Description and travel. 3. Poor--Education--Bangladesh--Dhaka. I. Title.

HV4140.6.D53M86 2009 954.92'205092 C2009-902402-0

Tangent Books, Inc.,
Box 51,
Hagensborg, British Columbia
V0T 1H0
Email: tangentbooks@hotmail.com

Tangent Books is a publishing concern of
Amarok Society
www.AmarokSociety.org
Email: info@Amaroksociety.org

All (100%) of the profits from the sale of this book are donated to Amarok Society.

Foreword

"Insanity is doing the same thing over and over again and expecting different results."   - *Albert Einstein*

Despite efforts to ensure world-wide education, which is the most powerful weapon against poverty, there remain millions of children too poor to go to school.

Most onlookers thought that a mother and father living in the world's most liveable city, Vancouver, Canada, were not of right mind moving their four children to the least liveable city, Dhaka, Bangladesh. Indeed, the Munro's have consistently opted to take the stairs.

The venture down this road not taken, against which they were warned, led to the opening of the innovative Amarok Society schools and effected positive change. The stellar concept of teaching mothers to teach their children and their neighbour's children is a unique model which can be cost-effectively and efficiently replicated anywhere in the world.

G.E.M. Munro transports us by rickshaw and literary prowess to the slums of Dhaka, Bangladesh, introducing us to the people of these neighbourhoods who work with little more than nothing to sustain life, learning, teaching and loving despite daily natural and not-so-natural disasters. The heroes, dedicated mothers who hold fast to hope amidst pain and loss, command the respect and love of the author, his family and the friends of Amarok Society.

The harshest and most blissful moments are made accessible to us. This inside look is not a staged version; **South Asian Adventures with the Active Poor** is jaw-dropping reality that reaches so deep we come away clearly aware that our fellow human beings transcend the seeming gaps between us. The Munro family's observations and experiences as delivered truthfully, humorously and lovingly by G.E.M. Munro, gift us gripping, revealing, touching and inspiring stories.

Amarok Society invites you to explore amaroksociety.org as active citizens of the world not doing the same thing over and over again, and achieving different results, supporting a service that offers hope.

Angela Macri, Chairperson, Amarok Society.

Introduction

Habib, our driver on a trip through the Bangladesh countryside, past rice paddies, past women drying rice on flat patches of clay, turning it over by scuffing their bare feet through the grains, walking back and forth all day, past men standing in channel water to their waists, beating jute stalks on the water, past flaxen jute fibres draped over bamboo fences and bamboo bridges to dry and age, past endless bamboo or thatched huts built on clay platforms surrounded by standing water, by men perched on little platforms affixed to poles stuck into channels, tossing and gathering nets, had a question for us, and he observed us closely in the rear-view mirror.

Actually, he had two questions for us; these were the pressing matters he needed to know from the first Canadians he had ever met. The first was for me alone:

"Brother," he asked in his extraordinarily gravelly voice, which had entertained us hour after hour with his tuneless, wordless singing, "you are Muslim?" And he motioned to his own chin to indicate my beard as the clue he pursued.

"No," I said, "just bearded." And just wishing he would return his eyes to the typical highway mayhem ahead of us.

He nodded in a tolerant, forgiving sort of way, and then chuckled, warm pebbles in a blender, as we roared around a shaggy little horse drawing a cart heaped tottering-high with round-bottomed aluminum cooking pots, past tiny corrugated tin and bamboo shops under large permanent signs, photographs of Bollywood superstars promoting skin-lightening cream. Habib was, I guess, letting The Force guide him, which is the only explanation for how we three, Habib, my wife Tanyss and

I, could still be alive after three days of his driving. Bangladesh has a vehicular accident rate 100 times that of Canada, one of the least mysterious statistics I've ever come across. Tanyss and I tried to reassure ourselves that Habib, by appearances, had already exceeded the life-expectancy of a poor Bangladeshi, so perhaps he actually knew what he was doing behind the wheel, against appearances.

We careened around three school buses, which are roofed cage affairs mounted on tricycles, in which brown children, beautifully un-lightened skin contrasting clean smock uniforms, sit facing each other on two sheet-metal benches, with Habib examining us more closely as he posed the really critical, really typical question:

"Sister, Brother, do you like my homeland?"

The question immediately transported us back to our homeland. When I've been to London, no one there has asked me if I liked it. In Edinburgh, they only wonder if they like you. No American has ever asked me what I think of New York, no Indian begs an assessment of Delhi. In Paris, their interest in you is limited to --- o, wait, there is no interest. But let the woman who finally cures cancer pass through Winnipeg, and the eager media reps will have but one burning issue to investigate: do you like Winnipeg? What do you think of Canada?

This, of course, springs from our innate sense of inferiority, which coexists in schizoid disharmony with our innate sense of superiority, and such is the case with Bangladeshis, based on a curiously comparable national circumstance.

Superficially, Canada and Bangladesh couldn't be more dissimilar: Canada is very big, Bangladesh is very small, about one eighth the size of Ontario; Canada is very rich, Bangladesh is desperately poor; Canadians have about the best quality of life on earth, Bangladeshis

2

about the worst; CA is very cold, BD very hot; CA has vast tracts empty of humanity, BD is the most crowded land on earth; CA's political system is relatively clean and accountable, BD was, for six years' running, ranked as the most corrupt nation on earth; at the time we moved from Vancouver to Dhaka, Vancouver was rated by the UN as the most liveable city in the world, Dhaka the least; Canadians are amongst the hardest-working people in the world and pride themselves on self-reliance, the BD press debates whether 'deshis' are the laziest and if it is becoming "a nation of beggars". Calgary was recently assessed by an international group as the cleanest major city, Dhaka as the second filthiest (Second? The assessors must have seen it on a clean day). If Toronto is New York as run by the Swiss, Dhaka is Kolkata leased out to Attila. If Saskatchewan is the land of the living skies, Dhaka is the city of the dead ones, where breathing is an act of slow, reluctant suicide. There's no place on earth less like the idea of Canada than the reality of Dhaka.

However, consider key psychological similarities: BD was a colony of a distant power that regarded its population as inferior rustics, at best, and it moved directly from that status to that of inconsequential little cousin of an inescapable giant neighbouring nation that: dominates and exploits it economically; floods its own culture with 'cultural' exports with all the depth and value of tinsel; claims to have won its significant war for it (perhaps correctly); is either sneering, scolding or dismissive; incessantly screams for its attention like the spoiled brat at the birthday party.

In other words, there is much about being a Bangladeshi to which a Canadian can closely identify. When Bangladesh beat India in a match of the last World Cup of Cricket, any Canadian would have had no difficulty understanding the excessive ecstasy the win induced, and

3

would have found something familiar in Indian television commentators, transmitting across the border, insisting that the result was due to what India failed to do, not what Bangladesh did.

Dhaka is the world's fastest growing city, and its most densely populated. It has five times the people Toronto has, and is expected to be the second largest city by the year 2020. Its growth, however, is almost entirely by the migration of the very poor from the countryside, hoping for opportunities that don't exist, and by their stunning fecundity. (Since their independence thirty-five years ago, BD's population has tripled. It is now so crowded that, if you took all the people in the world and put them in the U.S., the U.S. still wouldn't be as crowded as BD is. If you brought everyone in Dhaka down to ground level, each person would have one square foot on which to stand.) Dhaka surely remains both the least known and least cosmopolitan major city in the world.

So the answer to Habib's, and every Bangladeshi's, question was obvious. When first we came here, we would lie politely, o, yes, we liked it quite a bit. But in time, and as we came to know the land and its people better, we moved past politeness, and answered honestly.

This was, after all, the place that had given both of us dengue fever, a recurrence of which would have us weeping blood.

So Tanyss didn't hesitate to answer for both of us.

"We love Bangladesh," she said. "We love it with all our hearts."

Bangladesh is the world's largest delta. It has been formed and reformed through the ages by the deposited silt of great rivers flowing from the Himalayas. Thus the land is very flat, fertile, but not cohesive. The same rivers that made it, and upon which its people utterly depend,

4

also bring frequent ruinous floods, or devastating erosion. The Lord giveth, and the Lord taketh away? The Brahmaputra, then, is a most lordly river. Because the land is so flat, it is subject to disastrous typhoons and tidal waves coming north off the Bay of Bengal. Torrential monsoons can have an observer believing that BD is nothing but a few raised clay walkway strips in a nation-wide swamp.

How can anyone love such a land?

When Tanyss and I were living in Saskatchewan, we would talk to farmers, and nothing was ever right with them; it was either too wet or too dry, too hot or too cold. And the fact is, they were always right, it always was too much one way or the other. Do they love their province? How could anyone love such a land?

We lived in the arctic with the Dené, huddled beside the killer Mackenzie, under the killer cold, with a people who'd a history of cyclical famine. Do they love their land? How could anyone?

We've lived in a Quebec snowbelt where the drifts reached to the rooves, and shovelling was a career, and on an island in the Pacific where the rain began in September and never let up until one memorable day the next June. How could anyone love such a land?

Habib lowered his eyes from the mirror. Tanyss had given the correct answer. He rasped that chuckle of his again. He was a staff driver of the international aid organization that had brought our family (Azien, 18, Gabriel, 16, Grace, 12, and Alastair, 5) to BD. Under the strict hierarchical rules of the organization, he'd been ordered not to presume any fraternization with its professional officials such as Dr. Munro; it had taken Tanyss about ten seconds to dissolve his adherence to that absurdity, and now he sat with us at the roadside tea stalls and restaurants, and he called her the common address of "Sister", but I think, from his solicitous and affectionate treatment of her, she was as his favourite little sister, and, as for me, he'd hoped I was Islamic because he worried for the eternal soul of a brother about whom he cared.

We could have elaborated; we could have said how completely we'd come to love a people of such warmth, graciousness, generosity, humour, sincerity, of such determined, struggling goodness in the face of such adversity, how, as Canadians, we are predisposed to deeply love a people who deeply love a land that doesn't seem to love them back.

As will be repeated in the stories to follow, we observed that Bangladesh suffers under a most serious, and growing, problem: millions of children are too poor to afford anything at all like a proper education. We foresaw dire consequences to this situation, for the country and for the world. When we saw that other agencies seemed unable to respond appropriately, Tanyss and I, with the help of our own children, started our own, or, rather, revived a charity we'd begun years before, Amarok Society (often referred to herein as AS). After a few impracticable attempts to operate schools directly for acutely poor children, we hit upon an idea for a far more sustainable and expansive programme: we teach their mothers to be teachers of their own and neighbours' children. There are many reasons why this method is successful, nearly as many as why it's almost impossible, and they are discussed in a general way on our website, www.AmarokSociety.org. How we ever defied all advice and prediction, and actually went where we couldn't go and did what we couldn't do is another story, or parts of the several stories, included here.

When we were preparing to come to Bangladesh, the women at the international travel clinic who were repeatedly failing to get our rabies inoculation bubbles nicely rounded beneath our skin, and who, presumably, encounter conversations of world travel all day, couldn't quite place Bangladesh, mislaid its 150 million people, thought it might be part of India. That it certainly isn't: Islam is a very different religion from sensuous, celebrative Hinduism, and cloaks the obvious Bangladeshi culture in a grey-brown mantle like the Dhaka sky; I've never had any reason to doubt the devotion of the Bangladeshi Muslim; still, grit-toothed Bedouin austerity ill-fits the national character and spirit; like a properly-applied rabies inoculation, the colour, the joy, even the sensuality bubbles just beneath the surface, and we've been its fortunate observers. The following collection of tales is about a teeming people in what is the poorest region on earth, both in absolute numbers and in the percentage of the overall population, in a land that is little known, and little credited, beyond its bursting borders. If the stories don't demonstrate what it is about these people that causes us to have such respect and tender feelings toward them, the deficiency should be regarded as mine, not theirs.

Introduction (Ours)

The pretty young Bangladeshi woman behind the lost-luggage desk wore an attractive saree and radiated a professional air.

"You're moving from Vancouver to Dhaka?" she asked again in an educated English accent.

"Yes," I affirmed again.

"You're moving from (pause) Vancouver to (pause) Dhaka?" Her helpful manner was gone; her lip curled with distaste; she looked at me as though I were someone whose lost luggage, if it were worth finding at all, would be better than I deserved.

And I realized that her question was rhetorical.

"About our lost bags," I prompted.

"If you have a lot of bags, they'll sometimes leave some off and send them on another flight. You had six bags."

"Six bags for six passengers, one bag per person, the same as everyone else, according to my arithmetic; perhaps British Airways works it out differently," I allowed reasonably. "We Canadians are on the metric system."

Arrayed around me stood three small men in lungis, their hands resting on luggage carts in various states of disrepair and dysfunction, their eyes resting on the three bags we'd found. By my Canadian arithmetic, that was one bag each for me and my two teenaged sons, Azien and Gabriel, to carry.

"No taka," I said again to the men, but they shook their heads in disbelief, too; at least theirs was affable incredulity.

The young woman dismissed me with the information that we'd be required to return the next day to try again for our luggage, but to do that, we would have to obtain an admission form from the airport police.

9

When specifically asked, she curtly directed me to the police office.

"Did you notice anything ominous in her reaction to what we're doing?" Tanyss asked me as we went.

"O, I don't think so," I said. "Not necessarily."

"Nothing similar to the reaction you'd expect from, say, crafting origami pigs from the pages of The Qur'an?"

"I'm hoping I simply remind her of someone she despises," I said. "Maybe I sharply resemble someone who swindled her father and beggared her family."

"Holding to the optimistic possibility," Tanyss said, "or would that be 'clinging'?"

For the international aeroport of a city of a population nearing 15 million, Zia was a small, shabby facility, like three Yellowknife aeroport terminals laid end-to-end and allowed to go mouldy, so we had little difficulty finding the police office. The men with the carts followed us, darting forward from time to time to grab at one of our bags. No taka, I told them. Yes, boss, they told me.

Four or five uniformed men sat inside the office. I addressed our problem to the man sitting behind the desk piled with papers. As he riffled through a pile for the proper form, he became the first to ask the constant question.

"What is your homeland?"

"Canada," Tanyss said.

"Canada?" asked another officer, straightening up. "I want to go to Canada."

"Do you?"

"How do I immigrate to Canada?" he asked very seriously.

"No, no," said the officer sitting at the desk, holding up a hand to hush him.

10

"I mean it," he said intensely. "How can I go to Canada?"

Tanyss suggested he go to the Canadian High Commission to apply for a visa.

"No, I mean really."

The officer at the desk smiled at us uncomfortably, apologetically. "Sorry, sorry." He turned to the other. "No. That's not right."

The other, however, was determined.

"How do I really get to Canada?"

It gradually dawned on me what his insistent question actually was. We were already aware that Bangladesh had, for five years, held the title as the most corrupt country in the world, according to Transparency International. In Bangladesh, we were to be told, there is the official way, and then the real way.

In his eye there was a desperation very unlike our own temper in deciding to depart our country.

"I'm sorry," I said. "I don't know of any other way."

With our admission form in hand, we went to await Nuru, who was to meet us.

"Okay, perhaps this isn't the most encouraging beginning, all in all," I admitted to Tanyss.

She said: "Did you notice how the flight attendant kept checking with me that we weren't connecting to another flight, as though he must have misunderstood me?"

"What bothered me was the way the crew said good-bye to Grace as though she were the sacrificial virgin."

"The what?" Grace asked behind me. I cast a protective paternal glance her way. At twelve, she was reed thin, and her beauty seemed to emphasize her vulnerability. Holding her hand was her little brother,

Alastair, seeming very small and delicate at five years old.

"A very special version," I said.

"What does that mean?"

"O, you know... differing greatly from the ordinary version."

Nuru was a local employee of the international aid organization that had hired Tanyss to try to insinuate improvements into the standard of Bangladeshi education, and also to try to revitalize a regional office the head office thought defeatist and adrift. We'd never met Nuru, but we didn't expect he'd have any trouble finding us; we were the only white people in the aeroport. (Actually, we aren't an entirely-white family: our son Azien, eighteen at the time of our arrival, is a Dené Indian. It is, I like to think, his air of dignity that gives him such a striking family resemblance.)

We'd been warned before we came that this was a most violent city, that we would be at particular risk, as anti-western feeling was running high since the war in Iraq, that, for our safety, we should confine ourselves to the small international/diplomatic area of the city, that we should steer clear of any mosques, avoid anyone in religious habit, and that we must assume a haughty demeanour to avoid general harassment. Oh, and don't drink the water or breathe the air.

Nuru intercepted us, bustling busily into the area in which he wasn't authorized to be, a man typically short, nice-looking, but atypically brisk and impatient. He wore the attire of a mid-level office worker, creased slacks and short-sleeved collared shirt. We were to discover that his primary occupation was negotiations, bluster and buksis, and doing what he wasn't supposed to do. Any international office that has virtuously proclaimed it won't participate in the unofficial system of graft and bribe

12

(buksis) needs a Nuru to participate in it without saying so. Whatever his unrecorded job description might have outlined, sailing past armed officers into restricted areas would have been included.

"Doctor Munro," he said by way of greeting. "Come, come, let's go."

Tanyss made an attempt to introduce me, and Nuru shook my hand in a perfunctory way, but his attention was elsewhere.

"A car is waiting."

When he ushered us out through the doors of the aeroport, it was to a scene that astounded: under an extensive canopy was a broad sidewalk milling with people all seeming wildly fervent about helping us with our three suitcases and carry-on bags, oh, boss, boss, here, boss, here, here, boss, boss, and beyond it a driveway jammed with jostling cars, SUVs and tiny trucks, all blaring their horns frantically, drivers shouting out lowered windows, and beyond them a broad, high grid-work fence on which were climbing hundreds of men and women, yelling, crying and stretching their hands through the spaces, and beyond them the torrential monsoon.

My immediate reaction was that we had arrived in the midst of a national disaster.

And so we had: the disaster is named Dhaka.

The only flat available to us when we came was far from the international area of the city, which is quite close to the aeroport. We were driven from one end of the Dhaka to the other, and driven to distraction. The driver of our SUV was clearly a maniac behind the wheel, but so, clearly, was every other driver, aggressively swerving and barging and usurping, a giant game of 'chicken' at top speed, horns blaring incessantly. Around us, two or three inches away from us, careened horrible buses all torn down their sides from battles with other buses, panels crumpled and flapping, painted Bollywood starlets promoting Pepsodent Tooth Powder horribly mutilated, and around them wove broken little taxicabs, splashes of odd colours covering grievous wounds, and roaring yellow-hooded, ornately-decorated trucks sporting bits of shrubbery in their rounded grills, and between those darted little green, three-wheeled, canvas-roofed taxis. Obviously, traffic lanes meant nothing, and red lights were mere unsolicited suggestions.

In the inside pocket of my jacket was my international driver's license. Well, I won't be using that, I thought. It was apparent that traffic functioned on a principle of presumed aggression and imposition; any inculcated Canadian courtesy would be contrary to all others' expectations, and would be catastrophic. Perhaps if I'd been from Montreal.... Whenever our car was, through traffic congestion, brought to a halt, usually within one inch of the vehicle ahead, immediately it would be surrounded by bedraggled children hawking illicit two-dollar copies of Hairy Potter and the Goblin of Fir, which I guess was some woodland fairy tale, or by the most unfortunate and disturbing beggars, other bedraggled starving children, starving old women, young men without eyes led into the traffic by children, people without limbs carried by gaunt young men, all tapping fingertips through car window streams, boss, please boss, please boss, fingertips miming rice-to-mouths.

Nuru had brought a little pick-up truck for our luggage, and a tarpaulin to cover the bags in the open back, but no cord to secure the tarpaulin, so an accompanying office peon was charged with the task of spread-eagling himself across the tarp to hold it in place, and there was the little truck ahead of us, rollicking from

14

wheel to wheel, the poor peon clutching on for dear life in the down-pouring monsoon.

The roads were lined with little shops and businesses, some in fungal concrete complexes three or four storeys high with signs over them such as Royal Golden Plaza, some rows of flat-topped little tin and bamboo boxes, and behind them, discoloured concrete eight- or ten-storey apartment buildings, laundry hanging re-soaked on little balconies, or row upon row of mean little huts as far as the eye could see through the deluge.

Almost anywhere we looked were faint echoes of home in the school-teacher cursive Bata signs.

And everywhere, everywhere, people, people, people, a teeming mass moving through the rain.

In my mind's eye, Vancouver never looked better. In my head's eye, Alastair never looked paler; in case that wasn't merely in contrast to everyone else I was seeing, I gave his sweaty little hand a reassuring squeeze.

After a long, confusing time, we followed the little truck down a very narrow side road, where people brushed by us on either side like Satan's carwash, and then through a gate held open by a uniformed young guard, into a parking garage that occupied the ground level of an apartment building.

The drenched peon began to unload our bags. He was a man in his mid-forties, who stood about five feet tall. He had broad shoulders and broad hands, and very bowed legs. Azien, Gabriel and I instinctively went to help him unload, but Nuru quickly waved us away.

"No, no, let Mosun do."

We protested.

"Take rest from your journey," Nuru insisted, but he yielded to the point of lending Mosun a hand himself.

He led us into the little elevator, the thrill of which proved to be as exciting as any ride at the PNE, enhanced by the risks being more genuine, crowded in with Mosun bringing a couple of suitcases. Crowding means nothing to a Bangladeshi; compared to a Canadian, his personal space is … actually, I've never seen that he has any personal space.

"That was some wet ride," I said to Mosun.

"No English," Nuru said, but Mosun smiled at me with chagrin and shook his head, nonetheless, and made a gesture of flicking the water from his brow. We smiled and shook our heads in reply.

After a staggering stop at the seventh floor, we got out. There were only two flats per floor, and ours was the door on the right.

Waiting at the open door, possibly having been signalled by the guards below, was Beauty, a young woman who had been hired temporarily as our housecleaner. She smiled at us, but seemed more fearful than anything else.

"Nuru, ask her to bring Mosun a towel."

He did that, and she hurried to comply. Mosun seemed altogether too surprised and pleased when he was handed it.

We asked Beauty to make him a cup of tea.

Nuru took us on a tour of the flat, not that it was necessary; every room was obvious, and it was furnished very sparely. It was big, though, with four bedrooms and three bathrooms, including one for Beauty on the back side of the kitchen that was nothing more than a tap sticking out of the wall and an oval hole in a glazed clay platform. Beside it was her bedroom, just big enough for a narrow cotton mattress on the floor. The servant's quarters struck us as deliberately peevish.

Before he left, while Nuru waited impatiently, Mosun sought us out. To Tanyss, he raised his hand and said, very sincerely; "Sister, welcome! Sister, good-bye!", and to me, "Brother, welcome! Brother, good-bye!" and he did the same thing individually with our children. Nuru wasn't correct in saying that Mosun had no English; he had very little, but he drew on what he had to express to us what no one else had to that point. I was as grateful to him for that as he was to us for the towel and tea.

It turned out that we had both breached the hierarchical protocol of the organization; we went on doing that. Whenever Tanyss would see Mosun at the office, he would ask her, "How is my brother?" and she would answer, "Your brother sends his good wishes.", and when he and other office peons delivered some additional furniture a couple of weeks later, he had them gaping when he sat happily down, on the cane sofa they'd just brought, to join us for some tea. His two companions eventually joined him, perching at first as though the sofa might explode. It evolved that one of them spoke some English and enjoyed talking about politics, a very popular pastime here, and, through him, the three gave us a crash course in the critical matters of the day from their perspective. They were less than approving in their assessment, but they found encouragement and hope in the fact that BD leaders tend to die violently. They asked if Canadians cut short failing political experiments by the same practical expedient.

I started to tell them that a protester had once tried to strangle our Prime Minister, until I remembered that it was the other way around.

"Your Prime Ministers try to kill your people?" they asked.

"Oh, yes, always," Tanyss said, "but usually by boring us to death."

Being one of only two flats on the floor, ours had windows on three sides. Two sides were cheek-by-jowl with other apartment buildings, and on the third side, two more apartments were being raised.

On our first evening in the flat, the children succumbed early to their jet lag and were sprawled asleep on their lumpy cotton-packed mattresses. Tanyss and I were in the living room, very tired, but too wound up to sleep, so we sat in the lamplight and watched the little green-grey lizards on the walls and ceiling hunting little flies and moths, and then watched each other. We'd been through similar situations before, or, rather, situations so extremely apart, they were closing in on each other on the other side.

Suddenly, from the building right outside the living room window, there arose the most terrible, high-pitched feminine screaming. We rushed to the window.

Judging from the sound, the screaming came from a flat about the same level as ours. I believed I'd zeroed in on the very window, but it was at an angle to us such that I couldn't see anything inside it. The screaming slowly broke apart into spoken syllables, and then into a discernible phrase repeated over and over; of course, we had no idea what it meant, but it sounded desperately aggrieved.

There were instances during our years in remote aboriginal communities when we could walk along the roads of a village and hear nothing but anguish and woe coming from the little shacks. It was a dreadful marvel that an entire community should be in the grip of such unhappiness and dissolution. At the sound of the woman's wailing, we wondered if we'd landed into the same sort of thing, but to a multiple of 30,000.

A crowd of more than a hundred began to collect in the road outside the building, and several young men tried to scale a brick fence on the side of the building, to find a way into the apartment, I suppose, while other men and a few women pointed and offered suggestions. The tortured chanting continued, on and on, and then we could see, on the flat roof, several uniformed guards with flashlights peering around, shining their beams down each side of the building and discussing.

The screaming petered out more than stopped.

"What on earth have we come to?" Tanyss asked.

"This may be all right, actually," I said.

Tanyss looked at me in that way of someone who can't decide if fatigue has deranged her or the person to whom she's listening.

"All right as in 'The iceberg was relatively unharmed by The Titanic?'"

"No, this is encouraging," I said. "Look at all those people gathered down there, how concerned they all appear, how they tried to help. This doesn't seem to be normal, sweetheart. This seems to be exceptional."

The two apartments being built just off our dining room balcony were at differing stages of completion, so they provided an education in local construction, which was all bricks and concrete. Bangladesh, a country of clay, produces an awful lot of bricks. Brick kilns ring the outskirts of Dhaka, their ovens' fires fed by old tires, their black-belching smokestacks (brick, of course) like some vast Stonehenge from an asthmatic's nightmare.

Most of the construction labourers --- whole families, some of them --- camped in the unfinished buildings. Obviously, there were no facilities yet available to them, so they had to dump their waste into the patch of ground between their buildings and ours. Crammed right between the two new sites was a little old house, an artefact of how Dhaka had once been, and behind the house was a small vegetable garden that was surely receiving far more fertilizer than its gardener would ever have wanted. The stench was horrible, especially after one of the frequent monsoon torrents. The labourers couldn't be faulted; I'd see them early every morning at an outside hose, bathing carefully and washing their lungis and sarees, before collecting their skimpy breakfasts of rice. Their little nests, in plain view on the floors yet without walls, weren't slovenly; cleanliness mattered to them, and they were trying to live decently.

Bangladesh has very little in the way of gravel, so aggregate for the concrete is created by breaking bricks with a heavy hammer; this tiring, tedious task was often the work of children, crouching atop the red hill they were making. Young boys also spent the day pounding with hammers to straighten the long, bent rods of rebar used to reinforce the concrete, always without any protection for their ears against the clanging and ringing, or would cut the bar with a rotary saw, sending showers of golden sparks around them, without eye protection, just as older boys would later arc-weld the rebar without wearing visors. There were no derricks at these sites, no construction elevators; everything that went up the storeys, bricks, concrete, was carried up on labourers' heads. Women worked as hard as the men, climbing up the worrisome bamboo ladders and gangways, or carrying pans of sand, cement or broken bricks to the mixer all day, but where the men, in the oppressive heat, would remove their drenched shirts, and wrap up their lungis so that they were wearing no more than shorts, the women had to remain fully draped in their sarees, the extending shawl wrapping their heads. There is a cruel inequality for which a remedy isn't readily apparent.

20

We came to know some international people whose government or agency had paid to transport almost their entire household from Britain, or Holland, to Dhaka, as though anyone's Ikea sofa is irreplaceable. (There are some famous charities to which we'll no longer donate a dime, having seen how well-meant donations are squandered on the perfect comfort of its officials.) To its credit, the agency that hired Tanyss wasn't of that practice, and we had to select with great care what would be going into our one suitcase each. Tanyss and I'd had a mild debate about the merits of using precious space in Alastair's bag for certain Franklin the Turtle items, a few books and a big stuffed turtle that may not have been an authorized Franklin but sure looked like him, and a smaller Franklin toy decked out in a hockey outfit, including stick, helmet and skates; Tanyss' position was that Alastair was, at 5, pretty much beyond Franklin already, and we should be using the space for more mature material; my position was that he and I had bought the larger Franklin when he'd been 3, at a thrift store we went into while waiting for Grace to finish her ballet lesson one sunny Vancouver Spring evening, and how he'd toddled up to the sales counter to politely ask what it cost, and how thrilled he'd been to discover from me that 25 cents was an acceptable price, and that if she thought I was ready to let go of that Franklin, she had another think coming, but my stated position was the rationale that Franklin was Canadian, and Alastair could still benefit from the wholesome Canadian ethos Franklin imparted. Franklin's Canadian? Tanyss asked. Oh, yes, I said decidedly. He'll find no trace of Franklin in Bangladesh. I must put my foot down on this matter.

When we unpacked our bags, we found that our little travelling alarm clock would wake up no more, not even itself.

As mentioned, the flat in which we were stowed was far outside the safe zone as prescribed by Tanyss' office. Their answering precaution to this seemed to be that they would send a car everyday to get her (until they just forgot about it and left her to take a rickshaw), and that the rest of us, I guess, would just stay locked up in the flat, which was about as likely as turning on Bangladeshi TV and finding Franklin cartoons.

Our first full day there, Gabriel and I headed out to buy a replacement for the defunct clock. We soon discovered two important facts: that the roads of the neighbourhood wound around without plan, apparently just jogging any way through buildings already standing there; and that streaming Bangladeshi pedestrians don't think it rude to stop and stare in shock, and even point, at passing foreigners. Somehow, we found our way from our meandering road to the intersection of two main streets, and there we found a sort of market, a warren of little shops arranged on dark passageways. As we passed through it, we collected something of a retinue of shop hands who'd come out from behind their cracked display counters jumbled with salwar kamees or odd electronic bits or pirated Bollywood DVDs or things I still can't identify, to more closely explore the phenomenon that was us. We came to one shop stocked with cheap Chinese gimcrack, and on one of its little shelves was a really kitschy little electronic clock with a spindle that rose out of its main body to support a little plastic oval that waved back and forth. A small sticker on the clock said "300t". The shopkeeper was a young man wearing a long shirt and prayer cap. As our retinue crowded around, I pointed

22

to the clock and said to the young man, "Three hundred taka?" He nodded gravely.

That was about five dollars Canadian. I pulled a bunch of the weird money out of my pocket, and gave the young man three one-hundred-taka notes. He took the clock from the shelf, and as he did, someone from the crowd spoke to him.

"Three hundred!" the shopkeeper replied, his eyes wide with unbelieving elation. "Three hundred!"

Through the crowd and down the passage, the amount was exclaimed and celebrated, "Three hundred! Three hundred!"

The shopkeeper bundled the clock in a small paper bag fashioned out of an old official form of some sort, complete with fountain pen signatures.

As we made our way out to the main street again, yet more people appeared around us, eyes sparkling with merriment.

"Into the volley of derision rode the three hundred," said Gabriel. "Really, they could wait until we're gone, at least."

"So now we know how it goes. I declare," I declared, "such a thing will not happen again."

I soon had an opportunity to exercise my new haggling resolve, later that very afternoon, when the doorbell of our flat rang. I was in the living room, trying to figure out why a clock's plastic oval stops waving.

Beauty, who'd been mainly hiding from us, hurried to answer the front door, and, in a moment she appeared in the living room, shyly motioning me to the door.

Standing at it was a young man holding a pen and pad.

"Satellite TV monthly bill," he said.

We'd turned on the TV set in the living room out of curiosity, and had picked up only one ghostly channel of what appeared to be very old Bangladeshi melodramas, all set in hutted villages where handsome women swooned, handsome men wept, grinning goofs fell down hilariously, and wicked, bent men sneered.

"How much?"

"Twelve hundred, sir, monthly charge. Many foreign programmes."

"Too much," I said.

He smiled with deep personal regret, shaking his head. "Sorry, sir, set charge. Twelve hundred."

"Yes, well, I have a set charge, too, and it's on a short fuse," I said, and I started to close the door.

He held it open with his foot.

"Sir, no satellite signal," he warned.

"Yes, that's fine," I said. "I don't really want TV."

He seemed to be genuinely shocked. "No TV?"

"Not at twelve hundred, thank you." And I pushed the door closed, but I didn't bother to step away.

The bell rang; I waited a moment before opening the door.

"Sorry, sir. Set charge. Ten hundred monthly charge."

"Seven hundred," I said.

He looked at me as if I were strangling his grandmother.

"Oh, no, sir. No, no."

"No TV," I said, closing the door. "Thanks anyway."

"Sir, eight hundred," he said hastily.

"Seven."

He winced. He put his hand to his brow in the agony of what I was doing to him.

"Seven?" I asked.

He was too distraught to speak. Finally, he tilted his head to one side.

I gave him seven hundred taka. He made a notation on his pad, then presented it to me with the pen.

"Please, sir, sign."

"I mean seven hundred every month," I clarified.

"Of course," he said, suddenly recovered.

"How long will it take for us to receive the signal?"

"One minute only, sir," he said, pointing to a small plastic box on the wall outside our door.

He smiled and shook my hand with real warmth. We had a friendship forged in adversity...against each other.

Word of satellite TV spread as quickly through our flat as, o, the price of a crummy clock through a market. Azien and Alastair were already sitting at the set when I re-entered the living room.

"That's how you haggle," I said generally, in a tone that might be misinterpreted as smug.

Azien turned on the TV.

Why did we hear Bruce Cockburn singing?

"A Franklin cartoon!" Alastair said.

"Why, so it is. How delightful," I said in a tone nothing like smug. "Don't mention this to Mummy."

Thereafter, whenever I passed the tiny shop where I bought the clock, the young operator in his long shirt and prayer cap would rush out to invite me in; it wasn't to further exploit my foolishness, however, it was to offer me a little cup of coffee. I accepted his invitation a couple of times, and nothing was expected of me. We simply enjoyed each other's company in partially-understood exchanges. It seems he knew someone who'd somehow gone to Boston, and, as I was from Canada, I'd possibly heard of him. Had I ever heard any news of a Bangladeshi man in Boston? I tried to explain that a Bangladeshi dropping into Boston wouldn't cause the ripples of a Canadian dropping into his market.

I didn't visit with him more often, but only because I didn't wish to drink up his famous windfall profit.

Beauty was from a poor neighbourhood quite like the one in which we were now living, as homogenously Bangladeshi, and we were the first foreigners with whom she'd come in contact. That she'd hired on as our housecleaner was possibly simply the desperation of her poverty, or it may have been daring, courage. If it were courage, it seemed to have betrayed her when the abstract became the fact, and she spent her first days with us lurking and hiding. She seemed to be afraid to go out into the neighbourhood, too, so we ended up doing our own shopping for food, which we'd then leave on a counter in the kitchen, and then she'd cook us our dinner. It was known at Tanyss' office that she was capable of only one meal, curried chicken with rice and a lentil soup-like dish called dhal. This was the whole culinary library of many Bangladeshi women of her stratum, as they'd normally only have rice and dhal, and then very occasionally chicken or a fish called hilsa, a national favourite for reasons more to do with its availability than any other merits, I have to say. I found myself getting rather sick of the same dinner, until I considered having the same meal every day without the chicken.

In our explorations, we came upon a store proclaiming itself the first modern, western-type supermarket in Dhaka, betraying an inexact understanding of the model. It was called the PQS, which, it advised, stood for Price Quality Service, but we, for very obvious reasons, referred to it as Pretty Queer Smell. It was so western, it was playing a Christmas album on its scratchy p.a. system when we first went in, which was in July.

As we roamed its aisles, we became aware that we were being closely followed by young men in white shirts and black trousers. I nodded to them, and they nodded to me, and I didn't think much else about them; however, Azien, when a little Indian boy, had had too many experiences of going into stores in racist white towns on our travels, probably stores that had, by custom, made it clear to local Indians that they weren't welcome, to find himself, as honest and honourable a boy as there was, tailed by managers or clerks who made no disguise of their surveillance; some even went so far as to state "I'm just making sure this Indian kid doesn't steal something." So when these young men trailed around after us, he became angrier and angrier. At one point, he picked up a bag of chanachur, a spicy snack of peanuts, fried noodles and other things I don't want identified because I like it, and he glared defiance. Suddenly, one young man sprang forward. "Please, sir, may I help?" And that was all any of them wanted; just to be sure we weren't burdened by having to carry anything. Where they'd ever gotten the idea that such a level of service was to be found in a western supermarket, I couldn't even guess, but we decided against correcting their misunderstanding. (We'd heard people, several times on the street, trying to puzzle Azien out, this well-dressed, poised fellow. The usual conclusion: "Japon. Japon.")

As Beauty gradually became more confident with us, she came, by quiet means, to demonstrate what a poor shopper she found me to be. She would shake her head with regret over any masala I'd bought on her instruction, or the freshness of the chicken I'd selected, lifting a leg and letting it fall, as if to show that it was too, too dead; as a matter of fact, she might have bought a live chicken from a tiny poultry and egg stall just down the road from our flat any time she'd wanted, or from the poultry peddlers who wandered the neighbourhood, singing out, live chickens in baskets balanced on their heads. I think my lentils were always faulty, too, perhaps being too round, or too flat, and the rice I'd buy, well, dear, o, dear, not nearly ricely enough. It occurred to me that men simply aren't permitted to succeed within the feminine domain.

I approved of her, however. She did a good job of cleaning, and, aside from her silent censure of my domestic arts, she was very sweet in her shy way.

I found that I have a problem with household servants, that there are some things I can't require them to do, such as washing my laundry or making my bed; so Beauty, being conscientious, and, I think, wanting to prove her worth, entered into an undeclared contest with me, to see if she could get to my unmade bed before I could, sometimes possible because Tanyss generally sleeps later than I do, or could grab my laundry before I could wash it; I began to suspect that she was going into my dresser and taking clean laundry to wash, just for the points scored.

One afternoon, when Grace was overcome with a headache from the heat of our un-air-conditioned flat and took to her bed, Beauty sat beside her and stroked her forehead for at least an hour. She gave every impression of doing it out of kindness, not duty. That cinched her with me.

Tanyss' office director informed her that they were looking for a proper housekeeper for us. What about Beauty? she asked. No, a housekeeper, who can also cook, he said. Beauty's just a cleaner. What will happen with Beauty then? she asked. We'll let her go, of course, he said.

One of the errors of the office was the cavalier way in which it dropped low-level local employees back down to the terrible poverty from which they'd been elevated. We knew that Beauty's parents and siblings were depending on her puny pay. Tanyss told the director that we wished to retain her as our housekeeper. Impossible, he said. My husband will teach her how to cook, she said. Ludicrous, he said. You can't teach a cleaner how to cook! If it is ludicrous to try to raise people's skills and achievements through education, she asked, why am I here? You can't teach a grown woman from that level, he insisted.

We've had, in our lives, several instances where, if we'd simply embraced the opinion of jaded experience regarding our own and others' limitations ---- those kids can't manage an academic programme ---- you can't cure a gas-sniffer ---- our two races will never understand each other ---- you'll never be able to digest that ---- you can't teach a grown woman from that level ---- we'd have saved ourselves decades of hard work; of course, I'm not sure for what we'd have saved ourselves, exactly. Golf, maybe. Come to think of it, that one about our digestion proved to be advice we really should have heeded, after all….

Anyway, Tanyss ignored him, and I undertook to save Beauty's job by teaching her to cook, which was an interesting process in that she'd decided that the best thing for overcoming our language barrier was for me to learn Bangla, where I felt the best thing for overcoming her career barrier was for her to learn English. As a bachelor, I'd taught myself to cook fairly well as a stealthy means of winning attractive young women with delectable dinners; when it proved to be a stunningly successful tactic, and I won the best of them, I was rather stuck with the task as an implicit promise of the

29

relationship, and through the years I'd become quite skilled. So there I was, once again impressing, if not winning, an attractive young woman with my prowess in the kitchen. Beauty was most excited by odd things: she was absolutely tickled that she got to smash garlic toes with the side of a heavy cleaver, would cover her mouth and giggle every time; she found the transformation of oil, mustard, egg and vinegar into mayonnaise to be an ageless, confounding miracle; popping corn was almost too thrilling for her to bear.

She learned more English than I did Bangla.

One day I brought home a bundle of chicken keema, or ground chicken, which the PQS butcher packaged by merely piling into a paper bag. (Dhaka had banned plastic grocery bags some years before, when too many of them ended up blocking the wretched sewage canals that run along the sides of the roads.) It was a soggy mess by the time I got it home.

I asked Beauty if she'd like to try a hamburger. Dhaka is the last major city without a McDonald's, a signal achievement I had no interest in undermining by creating a local demand, so I was of two minds about the offer. She wrestled with it, herself, clearly, but, emboldened by our culinary adventures to date, she dared to consent.

As a concession, I spiced the burgers with cumin and a condemned curry masala I'd bought in an error bordering on sin. As I was cooking all of them at once, the family's and hers, it seemed natural that she should join us at our dining table to eat it. We found nothing quaint or cute in her initial extreme awkwardness and unease in sitting down with us; of interest, however, was the unanticipated problem she encountered when it came to eating a hamburger. She was, of course, completely adept at eating by hand, as that was how she always ate,

30

but she would eat with her right hand only; eating a big juicy burger inescapably requires that the unclean left hand come into play.

I'd had an illustration of how seriously she took this prohibition when, in our early days in Dhaka, she'd needed some money to pay to a houseboy from downstairs. I happened to be passing to the right of her at that moment, and, for the first and only time, I committed the gaffe of handing her the money with my left hand. She wouldn't receive it directly into her hand, but quickly covered her hand with a bit of her shawl to take it. She carried it that way to the houseboy, who, I suppose, had to contend with the filthy lucre's contamination in his own way.

Even as she hesitated in this hamburger problem, it dawned on me. I was trying to think of its solution, when she resolved it with a survey 'round the table. She lowered her chin shyly, but smiled, and then she lifted it with both hands to take a tiny tentative bite.

She loved the exotic marvel, and as she ate it her manner changed. We've seen some strange things; how many times has anyone seen a hamburger transform someone into a confident, worldly sophisticate?

From then on, it was necessary that, whenever I made hamburgers, I made one for Beauty, too.

One midday, we were visited by Nuru, who came for the unnecessary exercise of seeing that we had no ACs, as he referred to air conditioners. I was in the throes of a book --- writing, not reading --- at that time, and I spent my days holed up in our bedroom, with our uncomfortable cotton mattress as my office chair, and a low rattan dresser at its side as the desk for my lap top computer. As we, indeed, had no ACs to relieve the summer sauna, I was dressed only in shorts; my suits hung in an old wardrobe, raising a bumper crop of fuzzy fungus that I'd hoped to harvest as an economical supplement to our diet, until it assumed the angry, vivid colours nature uses to warn of toxicity (marking nature as kinder, more ethical than Dhaka milk companies).

Nuru was Beauty's immediate superior in the rigid office hierarchy, and she followed him dutifully but pointlessly as he bustled from room to room, noting spaces in the brick and plaster walls where ACs might have been but weren't. I came out of my bedroom to greet him. He was in an agitated state even for him, and when he was ready to take his leave, he made the mistake of saying flippantly to me, "I'm going. You can go back to sleep."

O, foolish Nuru, to expect that the line of the pay packet always pulls the greater loyalty. In an instant, Beauty the underling became the protective mongoose. Her eyes and teeth flashed white.

"Nah sleep!" she snarled furiously. "Sir work!"

I think both Nuru and I took a backward step. Little Beauty glared at him with molten scorn. Flustered and shame-faced, he muttered an apology and scurried away.

I stood in grateful wonder as she reverted to a shy smile and withdrew to her quarters.

Of course, within a couple of days, Tanyss' office director informed her that the Beautification project was at an end, a cook/housekeeper was to be hired for us, and poor brave Beauty was to be thrown back down into abject poverty.

The cook/housekeeper turned out to be an excellent fellow, our dear, stalwart Ratan. Beauty we hired from our own pocket as his assistant, a losing strategy for me in our laundry and bed-making contest, as she thereafter became even more deviously devoted and unscrupulously scrupulous. She has, for instance, hit upon the stratagem of, once a week, removing the mosquito netting from the frame of our bed, washing it, and putting it back, a difficult task I maintain falls in a grey area probably outside our contest, but which she clearly believes scores full points.

Our first flat in Dhaka was on Road 48 (new) 32 (old), Section C of our neighbourhood. A Vancouverite would assume that Road 48 (new) 32 (old) runs parallel to Road 49 (new) or even 33 (old), but that's where a Vancouverite would be, and was, wrong. To begin, Road 48 etc. wanders unparallel to anything, but, also, Road 49 etc. might not even be in Section C; it might be in Section B, which a Vancouverite would incorrectly assume to be somewhere adjacent to Section C.

It's easy to get lost in Dhaka, but it's not easy to stay lost. At any point on any road, there are six to eight men just waiting to give detailed directions, sometimes in a near-language somewhat resembling English, and sometimes actually accurate. The briefest moment of hesitation will bring them helpfully springing toward one, even a fleeting quizzical look. I once made the mistake of trying to clarify in my mind whether Beauty had been requesting the purchase of a certain masala or merely criticizing the one I'd bought the day before, which brought several men rushing forward and, before asking the halting questions "What is your homeland?" and "Do you like our homeland?", giving me elaborate directions to what turned out to be a roadside kiosk that sold English-language Dhaka newspapers. Apparently, they had logically deduced my need by the observation that I was a) a foreigner and b) (new) e) (old) I carried no newspaper. Out of curiosity, I followed their directions, and out of curiosity, I bought two dailies.

One of the papers was absurd, of such Islamic vitriol that it reported that all-out American civil war over the invasion of Iraq was mere days away, and that the Aga Khan Foundation or somebody was preparing a noble assassination of G. W. Bush to satisfy the world's righteous outrage. The second paper, though, was a broadsheet that, while indulging exuberant reportage that may have exaggerated sensational aspects of its stories, provided a model of editorial reason and balance that newspapers elsewhere in the world, including Canada, would do well to emulate. Its columnists examined their subjects with admirable probity, erudition and depth (and also space). It wasn't unusual for one opinion piece to discuss the latest political machinations, featuring illuminating quotations from Plato, Shakespeare and Lincoln, while drawing apt illustrations from incidents of world history. We began to read it regularly. In a most tumultuous time of terrorism and extreme political and social disruption, it often seemed to be the sole advocate for the pawns suffering in the middle of the board. I recall one issue where the front page reported on a High Court judge's declaration that the rule of law was no longer in effect in Bangladesh, then, in its inside pages, repeated, with the addition of meaningful quotation marks, the official police report of yet another prisoner dying inadvertently immediately after arrest, reported on the latest heinous brutalities of an Islamic-extremist thug holding sway in the northeast corner of the country, mocking the government's insistence that no such terrorist existed, and, on the op-ed page, a banker contended that the country's garment manufacturing trade was the new slavery, worse than the old, because slave-owners of the past assumed responsibility for the health, feeding and shelter of their slaves, where the garment industry assumed none of that for their millions of young women starvation-wage workers; that was from a banker. The government of the day repeatedly

34

threatened the publisher-editor with imprisonment for sedition, which would, of course, be gleefully reported on the front page. We believed it to be the best source of information through a period that distinguished Dhaka, and Bangladesh, as the most interesting place in the world, in the Chinese curse sense of the word "interesting". The paper had a lovely antiquated flavour to it, too, in its staff reportage, with by-lines such as "From Our Special Correspondent in Khulna", and an old-fashioned, florid love of the English language producing lines like "The miscreant was sentenced in absentia, as he is absconding still." or "The aroused crowd dealt the malfeasant a right good thrashing." Shocking to a Canadian sensibility were frequent, casual reports of the hanging of convicts, or advertisements for luxury flats available to "Foreigners Only!", or, terribly, begging advertisements for young people dying for want of surgical procedures they couldn't afford.

The paper initiated a series of articles by guest writers, famous Dhakans explaining "Why I Love Dhaka". The first couple of articles seemed merely to list the very reasons other people would hate it: the pressing bustle, the noise, the smell, the filth, the traffic, the sense of impending collapse into chaos, framed in terms of 'my wild, crazy city'. Subsequent articles offered reminiscences of what the writers had loved about Dhaka before it had so drastically changed: mongooses slipping through gardens, magpie robins singing through the day, pond herons not yet wiped out by multiplying killer crows, groves of trees, clean lakes and skies, playing-fields, bungalows rather than multi-storey flats…. Some were so evocative, they created nostalgia even in me, but they were hardly the intended celebration of the new Dhaka, and the series just quietly died, by malnutrition, perhaps, or arsenic poisoning, or typhoid, or respiratory disease, or one of the myriad other causes of the low life-expectancy.

The day after we arrived in Dhaka, there came a ring on our doorbell, and, as Beauty didn't seem to be nearby, I went to answer it. At the door stood a woman whose cheap, faded cotton saree didn't detract from her striking good looks, rather Pre-Raphaelite, although much thinner and with darker colouring. Plainly startled by the sight of me, she said a single Bangla word to me, eyes directed to one side, and then crouched down on her haunches just outside our door, as though in exhaustion, resting her elbows on her knees and interlacing her fingers loosely before her mouth.

I'd taken the precaution of learning the Bangla phrase for "I don't understand", which is "Ami boozie nah". I was to use it often, despite the fact that each time its use felt like a demeaning declaration of my sobriety.

I said it. In response, she said the same word more emphatically, still looking aside.

As Beauty wasn't forthcoming, I shook my head and closed the door.

The next day, the same thing occurred. The woman said the same word and crouched down again. Again, Beauty was making herself scarce. The next day was a Friday, and Beauty's day off, and once again the woman rang our bell, said her word, and settled into her forlorn crouch. I closed the door again, but a few minutes later I peered through the peephole in the door. She was still there. When I looked again later, she'd gone.

She had such an air of patient dejection about her, she captured my concern. And in the general atmosphere of unreality of those first days, beginning with the 5 am calls to prayers sung out through static amplifiers from the unavoidable mosques that surrounded our building,

36

the woman's elusive meaning began to assume an almost mystical quality.

One early morning, just as the puzzle of her was running through my mind once again, a crow landed on the iron railing of our balcony where I stood. This South Asian house crow struck me as a surreal grotesque of the North American common crows we were used to, with its grey hood and larger beak. It turned its head to me just as the woman did, and appeared as though it were about to say a word, and I wondered:

if the crow and the woman were somehow strangely connected;

if I could find out the Bangla word for 'nevermore', and if I'd recognize it the next time the woman called.

It turned out that the crow and the woman were connected.

That afternoon, she came again. Again she said her word, eyes away from me, again she settled down onto her haunches, perhaps a thinner Pallas fallen from over my chamber door.

"Ami boozie nah."

And she said a new word: "Rubbies."

Now, if that didn't just sound like an unpleasant exchange from East Hastings St…. it almost made me homesick.

Wait a second, I thought….

"Rubbish?" I asked.

She said, sadly, "Gee, rubbies."

"Ami boozie," I said. I went and fetched the plastic garbage pail from under the kitchen sink, sending scores of cockroaches scurrying for their lives, some right up my arm.

She took the pail with what seemed to be weary resignation.

It was her job to collect the garbage from all the flats, and to dump it on a nearby section of road, from where it might, eventually, be picked up by a man with a small cart. I don't know if beggars are pegged lower on the social scale than those who deal with garbage and sewage, but if they are, they're the only ones who are. I don't think even rickshaw wallahs are so tainted, and sneering down on wallahs is a national pastime. This woman had about the lowest job there is, and the mystery of her purpose and her attitude were solved simultaneously.

One day I suffered the unreasonable cost of some imported Australian apples. They were about five times the size of the hard, little local apples to which we hadn't yet adapted our tastes. Alas, they did nothing to ease the yearning for a Canadian mackintosh, and gave us no improvement on the flavour of the local midgets, and we neglected them to the point that they aged and wrinkled, and Beauty sought permission to throw them out.

Gabriel and I were stepping out the door of our flat when we surprised the rubbish woman, who was picking the withered apples out of our pail and wrapping them in the part of her saree that came up across her chest and over her shoulder. At the sight of us, she flew away, possibly ashamed, possibly afraid I was about to upbraid her.

From then on, whenever I saw her, she couldn't bring herself to look at me at all.

We are an energetic family, and it was our habit to use the stairs instead of the elevator, especially after our stimulating introduction to its erratic operation. This peculiarity of ours troubled the young guards and the smiling houseboys who spent their days with little to do in the parking level of the building.

One day, as Tanyss and I started up the stairs, the boys called to us and motioned for us to come back. When we did, one of the boys, with helpful exaggeration, showed us how to push the button for the elevator, and when its door opened, he showed us how to press the number of our floor. It would seem they'd surmised that the technology, of which they now demonstrated a patriotic pride, hadn't yet arrived in Canada. They gave up on us, though, when we continued to use the stairs: clearly, we weren't advanced enough to deal confidently with the magic little room that made the world outside it change.

There was a slight detriment to taking the stairs, as the little green lizards, called ticky-ticks for the noise they made with their throats, liked to hide under the flat metal handrail during the day. They had soft skin and wriggled as though my touch were acid when I'd happen to close my fingers on them. People here have affection for the ticky-ticks, and, although I had some issues with the diligence of their cockroach control, I didn't want to hurt them.

So I was climbing the stairs one day, between the fourth and fifth floor, with my attention too focussed on not gripping the handrail, when I was almost bowled over by a girl of about eleven who came barrelling around the fifth floor landing and down past me. She was as thin as the rail and very pretty, and she was the spit of the rubbish woman in miniature, with this telling variation: she was laughing, her face bright and happy. Even the partial blockage of an unexpected foreigner didn't interrupt her beam. She squirmed by me, and carried on downstairs at reckless speed, and, in another moment, the rubbish woman herself came racing down, chasing the girl, just as happy, laughing like sparkles on a stream. She faltered for an instant at the sight of me, but the momentum of her happiness carried her quickly by me. I turned to watch her, reflecting her bright beam, and as she turned at the lower landing, she looked up and shot me a laugh, a shared story between parents who have such simple delights in their children.

When I next saw her at our door, we smiled that story again. Thereafter, I seldom saw smiles, but her air of dejection was gone ---- perhaps the downcast eyes had been implying deference or lack of presumption ---- to be replaced by a direct demeanour of dignity. It became clear to us all that the rubbish woman's low status was in no way justified by any trace of stupidity, laziness or misconduct. She was where she was because that was where she was born. Her daughter, too, probably similar in innate intelligence and character, was certain to be deprived of an education, would find no greater opportunities than her mother, was destined to a life of scorn and relentless need, and old cast-off apples when she's lucky.

Everywhere we've gone, we've encountered the theory of the undeserving poor, that people in poverty choose to be there by their unwillingness to elevate themselves beyond it. The theory is rubbish too noxious for even that woman to dispose of, with all her occupational expertise. As we had seen so clearly in the past, and were to see time and again in the future, most poor people are poor solely because they are poor.

When we first arrived in Dhaka, we were very fortunate in that we were met with a situation most expats-diplomats-plutocrats would have regarded as very unfortunate; Tanyss' country office had been remiss in its preparations for us: our first residence was far from the "safe" international area, our household employee wasn't from the office staff of practised professionals. Our

40

introduction to Bangladesh was to be booted onto our own resources in the ragged, dirty, smelly, sad and funny environs most agencies pay a lot to encapsulate themselves against.

We were fortunate, too, that the recommended hauteur just isn't in our bag of tricks. We've never been harassed for want of it.

It has been our impression that, the higher, more official the dealings of the international person here, the lower his opinion of Bangladeshis. We have had discussions with reasonable foreigners who are utterly contemptuous of the people here, precisely the opposite of our opinion. We tell them they're mixing with the wrong class of people.

When we first were living in Dhaka, I didn't see anyone who wasn't Bangladeshi for a month, other than my family; I still distinctly remember the European man I saw on the busy footpath, so surprising was he; I'm sure I must have gawked with those around me, but I did manage to refrain from pointing. He seemed disappointingly sure of where he was going, and I had no chance to ask my burning questions: what was his homeland, and what did he think of Bangladesh?

Why I love Dhaka: well, I don't, we don't love Dhaka; no Canadian in his right mind could love "the world's new model of urban blight". But what of its people: are they the reckless perpetrators or pitiable victims of this disaster? The labourers of the buildings beside us were the producers of a stench so dreadfully penetrating, it would permeate our dreams at night, but they weren't its founders. We see the great majority of the people on a daily basis engaged in a struggle that would seem too discouraging to attempt. By our good fortune, our first dealings weren't with the official Bangladesh, or the "real" Bangladesh of graft and corruption, but the genuine society beneath those, the relationship of the people who, in the vacuum of official order and reliable institutional structure of cooperation, create order and structure of cooperation, continually save the land from the impending collapse into chaos not by fiat, not by obedience, but by deciding, one by one, to be honest, honourable, kind, dignified and decent, those with the warmth and yearning to reveal to strange blue eyes the common human heart beating within.

Alastair, the Heartbreak Kid

ALASTAIR

SITTY

TYING
THE NOT.

Alastair, the Heartbreak Kid

As part of Tanyss' work with the international aid organization that had brought us to Bangladesh, the painstaking effort to insinuate improvements into the extremely deficient public school system here, she was required to spend considerable periods of time in various villages outside Dhaka, and some members of our family would often accompany her, sometimes all of us. As always here, the numbers are stunning to a Canadian, and a village might have more than 200,000 people living in it, so more than most Canadian cities, but their atmosphere, somehow, remains rural. One village in particular became a favourite of ours to visit, a village eight hours by car and ferry (one hour as the crow flies, but nothing about Bangladesh is as the crow flies, unless the crow happens to be circling in on something rotten, of which there is much here) outside Dhaka. There is nothing much to distinguish this village from any others --- as with other villages, it is surrounded by extensive rice paddies that can, if one squints with determined intention, evoke southern Ontario fields when corn is still small, and sway-humped cows and bulls wander around the dirt streets, and, as everywhere in Bangladesh, the people are lovely --- but by circumstance we became integrated into it to a greater extent than to some others.

While there, we stayed in a tiny house with a little clay garden, through which myna starlings pecked with orange-framed, yellow beaks, through which pecked chickens, goats and dogs did small battles, and grey rats leapt in alarm at the sight of us, but not sufficient alarm to stay away. Tanyss and I shared our bedroom with (as well as occasional rats and toads) Alastair, who is six years old, and with Grace, who is thirteen; Alastair and Grace shared a bed, which resulted in much midnight teenaged protestation. Azien, nineteen, and Gabriel, seventeen, shared the other bedroom.

In the final days of the Bangladeshi war of independence from Pakistan, with the handwriting on the wall and the successful outcome for Bangladesh a certainty, the Pakistani army still within Bangladesh did something atrocious: they rounded up all the intellectuals, scholars, artists and poets they could find, and shot them all. This outrage, of course, wasn't for the purpose of winning the war, but was for the purpose of crippling the new country to emerge. Perhaps as a result of this well-known, annually-commemorated calamity, Bangladeshis have a respect and appreciation for intellectuals, scholars, artists and, most of all, poets that can be weird, head-spinning, unnerving to a poet from Canada, where "... can you eat a poem? Well, can you?" is, as I recall, a line from the second verse of our national anthem.

At the time of my first visit, when word got 'round this village, I suppose through Tanyss' staff there, that a foreign poet was staying there, many people gathered to look at me, and to assure me that the village is a very fine place to compose. As Bangladeshi poetry is, more often than not, bucolic in subject matter, they are probably right. On the last morning of our visit, several people gathered again, with the pressing enquiry: had I written a poem during my stay? I was able to report that I'd written not one poem, but two; a cheer went up from the group. Gabriel took the opportunity to whisper "If they had any idea what sort of poems you wrote....", but, still, it was heady stuff....

The village is remote enough that the occidental tourist never roves through, and our fair-haired children aroused a great deal of excited interest. Azien is dark, with colouring close to the local range of normal, so he was regarded more as a curiosity, with his tall stature and dignified Dené demeanour; but the local teenaged girls openly gaped and giggled over blond Gabriel and clamoured for the chance to brush Grace's copper hair, and generally bestowed upon them a celebrity no harder earned than Paris Hilton's. The real superstar of the family, however, was Alastair, of the bright blue eyes and curly golden locks, whom the people, even other children, treated as an adorable exotic marvel. We might have concerned ourselves about the effect on his ego, but Alastair seemed to accept his status as merely another oddity in an odd childhood.

We had a demonstration of Alastair's fame when Tanyss and I went for a long, long walk one late afternoon, through golden sun dappled by over-reaching mahogany trees, down a winding, dusty road past bamboo huts constructed on four-foot clay foundations, maybe up above the line of the inevitable floods, maybe, and ponds with ducks paddling in them and kingfishers, rich rust with shocks of electric turquoise, perched above them, and, hours and miles from home, after we passed two women silently watching us from the doorway of a hut, we heard behind us "Canada. Alashtore."

It became readily apparent during our visits that the most dangerous educational situation, as everywhere else here, wasn't that the schools were poor performers, but that many too many children of the village are too terribly poor to afford school at all, beautiful children whose tattered tee-shirts' legend of "for your birthday" with illustrative cartoon rabbit and cake with candles can just barely be discerned, darling bright-eyed children who don't know how old they are and have never had a birthday party, and have never heard of rabbits.

Numbers of them would collect around Alastair every morning in the garden, to play soccer with him or just idle away in his company, and one day, on a sudden impulse, I succumbed to my perilous intrinsic impatience with their situation and took a small white board out to the porch and sat down on the top step.

"What's this?" I asked generally, writing a big A on the board.

The children immediately collected close around me. None of them answered, of course; probably none of them knew what "What's this?" meant, but I reckoned that would change soon enough.

I took Alastair by the shoulder and placed him in front of me, and drew a little portrait of him. This had precisely the effect I'd expected; during our years in remote First Nations communities in Canada, children never ceased to be amazed by my ability to accurately portray, on paper or blackboard, an image in front of me or from my memory; they regarded it as a most mysterious magic, and, actually, so do I.

And so did these children. As the portrait took shape, they pressed more tightly around me and gasped and exclaimed most pleasingly. This was a bit dicey, of course, as fundamentalist Muslims still regard portraiture as leading to idolatry, and a sin, and our little house was surrounded by no fewer than four small mosques within a (gulp) stone's throw. But I was, as I say, impatient.

"A is for Alastair," I said, and I wrote the name under the picture.

I took one of the leaning little boys by the arm and positioned him before me.

"What's your name?"

He smiled uncomfortably and shook his head.

"His name is Alastair," I said, motioning to Alastair. "What is your name?"

His eyes lit up, and he said "Robeen."

"R is for Robeen," I said, writing an R on the board, and, beside the picture of Alastair, I drew a portrait of Robeen, then wrote Robeen below it.

A beautiful little girl slapped her bare chest with her hand.

"Suberna!" she said.

I held up a cautionary finger. "My name is Suberna," I corrected.

With only some hesitation, she repeated it, and so I drew an S, and a portrait of her, and so on.

And so on and so on, because more and more children crowded into the little garden, until there were dozens, all eager to say "My name is----" and have their portraits drawn, even though it was obviously possible only to preserve them for three portraits' time until they were erased to make space for new ones.

Grace, who's also adept at portraiture, joined me with another white board, and we became like two barbers or dentists side-by-side, except that the children didn't wince much at all.

Through the morning, all that representational depiction didn't lead to any noticeable idolatry; although I did get the feeling the children were becoming rather keen on us, I'm pretty sure it didn't approach idolatry.

When Tanyss came home from her nearby offices for her lunch break, she assessed the situation, and said, "So, are we starting a school?"

"Oh, no," I said. "We're just showing them some little things."

"Hm-hm," Tanyss said. "And at what point will we stop just showing them some little things?"

"Right now," I said, setting aside my board. "Let's go for a walk."

We hadn't gone very far along a pathway between the huts behind our house when a teenaged girl whose

48

open face radiated out from a black burkha caught up with us and shyly but firmly indicated she wished to speak with us.

"Please, my father's house," she said when we gave her our attention, and she motioned back along the path. "Tea. Entertain."

We get many invitations to spontaneous visits, and we've learned to distinguish various forms. "My father's house" is a phrase that implies an aspect of honour or dishonour, a more serious intention to the visit, and shouldn't be lightly refused. Anyway, the girl smiled so sweetly....

We consented, and she led us within a fenced yard and into a small home. In the front room we found her father, an elderly man of long wispy white beard and obvious self-possession and warmth. He was dressed in a crisp white long shirt and lungi and wore a clean prayer cap. He nodded with delight at our arrival, and motioned us to sit on a small bench, and he sat on a little stool. No mother was forthcoming, so we correctly assumed him to be a widower, but shortly we were joined by, and introduced to, the girl's, Samima's, slightly older sister, Sreboni, who also dressed in a black burkha, and who brought us small cups of tea. Samima's success had been expected, apparently.

After some standard courtesies and niceties, as carefully translated both ways by Samima, the old man began to outline his admiration for education, as manifest by his support and encouragement of the scholastic achievements of his two daughters, which he detailed. We congratulated him on his wisdom and progressive attitude, which gave him calm satisfaction, and then we congratulated the girls. At that, Samima smiled very widely, and gave meaningful looks to her father and sister. It was Sreboni who took it upon herself to address the critical matter at hand.

"Please, madam, sir, Samima and I wish to teach in your school."

"What school?" I asked.

"You do?" Tanyss asked.

"Yes, madam," she said, answering the easier question.

"What school?" I asked.

"You know, our method of teaching is different from what you've experienced," said Tanyss.

"Yes, madam. We have observed. We wish to learn your method."

Tanyss promised that we'd be in touch with them, and I asked why, and then we took our leave, and were barely out on the path again when we were met by Joy, a large, lovely man on Tanyss' staff.

"Big sister," he said, "we have found a hut for your school."

I have lived with two races of people who are supposed by prejudicial reputation to be lazy and incapable: Bangladeshis and Canadian aboriginals; and I say that if you want some unusual or difficult task or organization carried out quickly, efficiently and without fuss, turn it over to an aboriginal community or a Bangladeshi neighbourhood. That'll get it done, maybe even before you're aware you want it done.

I took one last stab: "What school?"

Tanyss confronted me squarely.

"Sweetheart," she said, "realistically, at what point will we stop just showing those children some little things?"

"Oh, realistically. You hadn't specified 'realistically' before." I turned to Joy. "So where is this hut?"

The hut took a few days of preparation, and Joy took the time to distribute and accept applications from parents and fill out forms perhaps having something to do with that (Bangladesh is the most highly-bureaucratized nation in the world, which suits its people just fine). The only qualification for the children was that they not be attending another school. From just the immediate circle around our house, we had a hundred applicants. The hut was going to burst at the jute seams.

One evening, as I sat on our front porch watching the little green ticky-tick lizards stalking bugs on the canopy overhead and stomping my feet when the rats came too close, Rubel, a very fine man and another member of Tanyss' staff, came and sat with me. I enquired about the well-being of his wife and six-month old daughter. He told me they were fine, but I knew it was only from hearsay he could answer. Like many young Bangladeshi breadwinners, his job had taken him far from his home village, but didn't pay him enough to allow his family to come with him. Rubel lived in a crummy little room he shared with Joy, and he had never seen his beloved daughter.

Joy and Rubel are of a similar degree of good-nature and humour, but where Joy is ebullient and his jokes exuberant, Rubel is quiet and his jokes dry and understated. But he warns of them with a half smile.

"Brother, all are asking why our big brother cares nothing for us," he said, half-smiling.

"What would lead you to believe I care nothing for you?"

"It must be. All are asking why you teach children you don't even know, but not your dear friends."

"I see. And which of my dear friends would like to learn what?"

"You know all your friends on our big sister's staff must learn excellent English to succeed."

"I don't suppose you already mentioned this to Tanyss," I said.

"She told us she doesn't know why our brother cares nothing for us," he said. "She told us we should ask you why."

"Did she just? And when did you hope to begin these English lessons?"

"Oh, not until tomorrow evening. Tomorrow evening would be fine," he said. "And then every evening. We've named our school the Munro University."

"Have you indeed?"

"Yes," he said, plainly pleased with the course of the conversation.

"Children you don't even know" had simply been a debating point for Rubel, and in no way represented the attitude of Tanyss' local staff to our little pupils. All of them happily and conscientiously undertook any means of helping us of which they could conceive, and would show up at the school frequently just to visit.

So it went; with the attention and assistance of sisters Sreboni and Samima, Grace and I would take half of our school's overpopulation and teach reading and writing while Gabriel and Azien took the other half to teach arithmetic, and then at lunchtime we would switch; in terms of heat, it would have seemed refreshing to take a respite in a coke oven (not that I really have that basis for comparison), but the dear little children never stopped coming to sit knee-to-knee, shoulder-to-shoulder on the woven mats, and the sisters never varied from their black burkhas; and then in the evening, after their long day's work but before their dinner, the sisters and Tanyss' entire staff would join us in the main room of our little house for a two-hour English lesson, often conducted by candlelight for reasons explained below.

The sisters were quick studies of what Sreboni called our "beautiful system of teaching", and when one of our stays in the village would be over, we were confident in leaving the sisters in charge until we returned.

Little Alastair took the role of teacher more than pupil those days in the little hut, helping the children sitting around him, and that did nothing to exhaust his celebrity in the village, as we shall see.

Our bedroom in the little house was also the school office, which amounted to a laptop computer on a chair by the edge of our bed. Bangladesh uses four different configurations of electrical outlets, which seems tolerant, even liberal, at first glance, but in practice reveals instead a typical lack of resolve; in other words, it's rather like the Bangladesh Constitution. As any electronic device has a three-out-of-four chance of not matching an outlet and never seems to beat those odds, we had jerry-rigged, suspicious adaptors plugged into suspicious adaptors plugged into odd power bars plugged into scorched wall outlets that clasped with less determination than disaffected former friends. The danger of these arrangements was, fortunately, mitigated by the fact that we had power blackouts totalling about 20 of every 24 hours. All Bangladesh has numerous blackouts every day, but this region is particularly susceptible because it voted for the opposition in the last election.

As people of the village are curious and not a bit shy, we'd had to get used to large groups of them collecting around our house or school, leaning in through doorways to watch us eat our meals, etc. Adults often included themselves in the school lessons, joining in with gusto in the singing of 'ABCD' and shouting out answers before the children could.

So it wasn't abnormal that a woman with a little girl on her hip should position herself in our bedroom doorway one afternoon as I pecked away at my laptop computer. Her manner was somewhat abnormal, however; usually, such imposers assume an expression of kind, patient interest in, or pity for the affliction of, my strange appearance, or perhaps an animated geniality (Bangladeshis live by the idea that a stranger is just a friend with whom one hasn't spoken yet), with eyebrows dancing to some cheerful internal tune. This woman, however, bore a sharp sort of glint in her gimlet eyes as she watched me. I smiled over at her briefly, but her severe manner didn't change. The little girl was an utter cutie-pie, with big watchful eyes under dark glossy curls; she was perhaps something over two years old, although she might have been older, as the usual diet of the people there, rice and lentils, is deficient of nutrients to the point of 'stunting' --- six-year-old Alastair towered over some ten-year-old boys. She was wearing a spanking new yellow sweatshirt with matching little sweat pants, which was most unusual. I smiled at her, and she tucked her little chin into the neck of her shirt. The woman issued a curt command, and the little girl, in response, began to salaam me, but she did it with her left hand; the woman slapped her left hand down and chastised her.

"Oh, that's all right," I said reasonably, even though for all its use I might have been reciting a defunct BC licence plate.

The woman barked another instruction, lifting the baby's right hand, but the tiny one had already ventured beyond the point of her confidence, and she tucked her hands away and wouldn't direct her large eyes toward me

54

again. The woman set her mouth grimly and looked at me as though to suggest it was my fault, somehow, so I turned my attention back to the screen of my computer and pretended to work in a way that would transmit the conclusion of our little visit, not that such social subtleties had ever worked before.

I poked away for about five minutes under her continuing scrutiny, and then, by way of concession to her determination, I looked over to them again. The woman made a downward pawing motion, which means 'come'. I shook my head, which means 'no', but she was dismissive of any opinion I might have in the matter. She yet lowered her hawk brows and motioned more emphatically, the very picture of a woman who isn't used to losing arguments. I, on the other hand, may lose arguments, but I don't always have to admit I do, so I turned my best expression of granite resolution back to the computer.

The woman withstood about twenty minutes of me ignoring her, then slipped away, and I foolishly assumed that I'd won our little battle of wills.

About an hour after the visit, Tanyss came to our house for a break and we decided to take a stroll. The village is situated on a river that flows to the Bay of Bengal. Parallel to the river is a long canal that joins the river a short distance south of the village. The sea is 400 kilometres away, but Bangladesh is so flat that, at high tide, the river and canal reverse and flow upstream with salt water. This salt water seeps into the ground water, so that water from wells is very saline; I thought I didn't like tea with sugar, until I had tea with salt....

On our walk, we decided to follow a path we came upon which traced the bank of the canal. We were soon skirting along little family groupings of corrugated tin shacks, when who should come skipping along to encounter us but the same little girl, still dressed in her new sweat suit, who'd been brought to visit me earlier. She smiled brightly, as though we were long-term friends, and salaamed me, again with the wrong hand, then turned and hurried back the way she'd come.

"Oh-oh," I said to Tanyss. "We've got to turn around."

I explained to her about the unusual visit and my suspicions regarding it, and surmised that the little girl would be announcing that I'd relented and we were coming to the woman, after all.

"Of all the paths to take," Tanyss said, but she might have said as much about our move to Bangladesh.

For all his woes, the typical Bangladeshi can have a merry manner, and is freely given to laughter and song, just as he is to prolonged lament, heated debate and verbose denunciation; there is little of constraint in the national character. An exception to this is presented by our cook in the village: her name is Hasi, which means 'laughing' and in her case suggests a parental optimism unfulfilled. Her demeanour is unusually self-contained and solemn, and very quiet. The most effusive response we can normally draw from her is a slight tilting of her head, a gesture that imparts respectful acknowledgement or gratitude. She is very poor, very thin and very pretty, and has four skinny, good-looking young sons, all of whom were enrolled in our school, and the eldest of whom is by reputation a mute, although I'm not completely convinced he isn't merely slavishly following the maternal model.

That evening, as Hasi was bringing in our dinner from her cooking hut (it was always the same meal, every noon and every night: small bony chunks of curried scrawny old hen, rice, and dhal, a spicy, wet lentil mixture, like a thick soup, with a few slices of cucumber. Hasi is, however, an artist of this limited cuisine, at least in that she uses it as her medium of self-expression: the more hellishly spicy it is, the angrier she is at me over something about which I am always clueless), she carried with it an air of mysterious observation even more unsettling than usual. And when, during the course of the meal, she silently, even stealthily, placed a lit lantern just inside our dining room door, my alarm bells pealed.

I went to the back door, and saw assembled there in the dimming light of the yard a group of a dozen women staring intently back at me.

Anyone who thinks that all Muslim women dwell in cringing subservience has never been to Bangladesh; the group gathered in our yard looked very much the fully paid-up local chapter of the awe-striking global sisterhood we first encountered in aboriginal communities across Canada, cohesive, confident and determined.

"Something's afoot," I said to Tanyss. I drew her attention to the solemn congregation, Hasi's curious placement of the lantern and benign restraint in her use of chilli and curry that evening.

When Hasi decided we should be finished with our meal, she re-entered the room and motioned cryptically to the women in the yard. Through the door came Ritka, a lovely teenaged girl who resides near us, who'd apparently been recruited by the older women for her very limited knowledge of English.

"You pleashe come walk Alashtore," she said to Tanyss and me. One of the women stepped forward and took the lantern.

"Where to?" I asked.

"Walk Alashtore," she said, taking Alastair by the hand and pulling him from his seat. She whisked him out the door in an instant.

Tanyss and I sprang after them. Outside, in the gathering dark, the woman with the lantern smiled warmly and motioned for us to follow Ritka and Alastair, who were disappearing around the corner of the house. We quickly caught up with them, and Ritka's pace eased down; the women collected around us, the woman with the lantern in the lead; she set a sedate, even ceremonious pace. In time, we crossed the concrete bridge over the canal, and Ritka guided Alastair along to the path we'd begun to explore that noon.

"Oh, no!" said Tanyss. "I know where we're being taken!"

"Oh, no," I said.

Our exclamations seemed to spur Ritka afresh, and, laughing back at us, she raced Alastair ahead, into the pitch black. How she could see her way, I've no idea. As we went, there came to us a multitude of voices.

"We'd better get a move on," I said, "or they'll have Alastair married before we get there."

Eventually, we came to the entrance of a lantern-lit courtyard surrounded by a woven rush fence and three bamboo-frame, corrugated tin houses, a sort of compound, which was filled with a large crowd of people, the originators of the multitude of voices, all of whom were turned in to observe Alastair standing at the centre, standing, I must say, with remarkable aplomb given his situation.

We went in and threaded our way through to our little boy's rescue. Ritka beamed at us with what I took for mischievous delight, and then there stepped forward a man of about 35 years. He was good-looking, upright and dignified, and he shook my hand with sincerity, introduced himself as Abul, and motioned for us to enter the central house.

Across the width of a narrow front room was a bed, and the man indicated that Tanyss and I were to sit on the bed. Alastair was sat down on an old wooden chair off

58

to the side, where he could remain the centre of attention. As many people as could crowded into the little room after us, and we could hear the remainder of the people talking excitedly, collected around the house, their voices travelling freely through the many open spaces in its simple construction. Abul placed a wooden bench before us, and there were passed in from outside three unmatched glass tumblers, which he then placed on the bench.

It soon evolved that our host knew about as much English as we three, together, knew Bangla, so we were able to manage a rudimentary communication.

"My mother mother," he said, proudly motioning to a woman sitting on an overturned bucket beside Alastair. She grinned at us toothlessly, her brown face crinkling inward. Given the life-expectancy in rural locales, she was indeed an ancient, and Abul had reason to be proud.

Everyone present settled into a silent atmosphere of expectancy, with frequent smiles and nods. In time, a grey-haired woman, unusually stout in a village of perpetual under-eating, moved with stateliness through the parting press of people, and came to stand at the forefront.

"My mother," Abul said with obvious respect.

It seemed it was she for whom we'd been waiting. We smiled at her, but her appraisal of us was frank and serious. Alastair stood to give his seat to this august personage; she protested, but his inculcated courtesy would allow nothing else. She settled into it solemnly, and I lifted Alastair over the bench to sit between us on the bed.

Then the other shoe dropped. The woman of my day's visit came forward, carrying the same little girl. She positioned herself directly before us. The little girl, coached to perfection, salaamed me properly.

Now, there can be a problem with Bangla names in English speech; one could recite French or Spanish or, probably, Vietnamese names all day without encountering any that caused discomfort to the English sensibility. Not so with Bangla names. For instance, our cook in our home in Dhaka is named Ratan, which is inescapably pronounced 'rotten', and our maid is named Beauty, which seems an awful lot to have to live up to; she makes it all the way to quite pretty, but, well, the discrepancy between the advertisement and the item itself is noticeable. As a family, we've admirably resisted the temptation of "rotten food" jokes, but every time we speak of Ratan and Beauty, we feel as though we're telling a tale from Grimm.

That sort of problem arose again when Abul introduced the sweet little girl as 'Sitty', which seems nearly all right in print, except that 's' is always pronounced 'sh' in Bangla.

"Hello, um, Sitty," we said in our best and most self-conscious Bangla pronunciation. Alastair looked up at us with quiet interest, and I widened my eyes, trying to communicate to him some caution I couldn't possibly.

The woman, as severe as ever, directed Sitty to look at Alastair.

Then Abul went to the door and brought forth a bottle of pop. Bangladesh is the land where copyright dies, and local manufacturers have fun naming their products in ways that will cause the utmost confusion with famous international brands. The bottle Abul brought was a lemon-lime drink labelled 'Ten Up'. He poured us each a drink of it, and then a girl brought in three bananas and placed them on a small table to my left. Then the pièces de resistance were brought in: three small bowls of whitish goop and three small spoons were placed on the bench. Abul was all proud smiles as he anticipated the impression this offering was sure to create, and his happiness was reflected in all those gathered around us. Even his mother softened somewhat in the shared warmth rising as wisps of steam from those bowls, those little demonstrations of the generosity, prestige and sophistication of the host family. Tanyss and I exchanged secret looks of direst dismay.

No greater proof could be produced of the long-term damage of colonial rule than the fact that rice pudding, probably the worst blight of British culinary shame, is still put forward as a high-class, edible concoction in Bangladesh sixty years after the end of the Raj era. To me, it's always been the dessert of old, old frail people who are convinced life holds no joy, and use rice pudding to confirm their pessimism. As my children will attest, I have referred to it as 'larva pudding', 'pudding your maggot where your mouth is', and 'bleached rat droppings in goo', and have often verified the benevolence of my paternal career against their contrary accusations by citing the fact that I've never once required my children to taste it.

Now, nearly two decades of kind, fatherly protection were about to go for naught: I leaned down to Alastair's ear and whispered, "This is very important to these people. No matter how disgusting you find the pudding, you must eat it." I believe my voice broke a bit as I put my little son's training as a gentleman to such a stringent test. I squeezed his shoulders in impotent reassurance; tears welled in his big blue eyes, but manfully he dipped his spoon into his hideous bowl. "Wait," I said, my heart heavy, "let me do it first." Mother and son turned to watch in fearful enquiry as I raised the despicable stuff to my lips. And, Allah be praised, it wasn't rice pudding at all! It was some coconut mixture that was really pretty good. I sang out the good news, but poor little Alastair was too traumatized by the mere anticipation to immediately recover: he keened softly for a world where rice pudding is even a possibility, realized or not.

More in relief than outright enjoyment, I announced all around how balo the pudding was, and everyone glowed with success. As we continued to eat it, it seemed that the people started laughing at us, laughing loudly. Even knowing of the normal cheerful national character, this seemed a bit much to me. I looked about in annoyed confusion as people pointed toward us and roared. I happened to glimpse a motion behind me, and turned to discover the cause of their hilarity: a very little boy, clad only in worn old shorts, had snuck up behind us on the bed, and had snatched two of the bananas from the little table beside me. He stood behind us, a banana in each hand, taking alternating bites, his cheeks bulging.

"Mister Bean!" Abul cried, and everyone, including all those gathered outside, hooted with laughter at the reference. Eventually, the boy finished the bananas, thoughts of Rowan Atkinson flew off, and the laughter subsided.

Still smiling, the people settled into silent observation of us.

In time, Abul was struck with an inspiration. "Please sing," he said. It's usual enough for guests or strangers to be invited to sing, but we are still western enough to happily shift that burden of response to Alastair, who'll sing at the drop of a hat.

"Alastair will sing," Tanyss said. "What will you sing, Alastair?"

"Twinkle Twinkle," Alastair said.

A look of solicitous concern clouded Abul's face. He spoke to two women, who immediately stepped forward, moved the bench aside, and led Alastair by the hand out of the house.

"Where are they going? Kodai?" Tanyss asked, but Abul smiled and raised his hand, signalling for us to be patient.

In just a few minutes, the women led Alastair back into the house. He came and sat once again between us.

"Will you sing now?" Tanyss asked.

"Yes," he said, and then he lowered his voice. "And if either of you need to use the toilet, I know where it is now."

I puzzled over that as Alastair sang 'Twinkle Twinkle', until it occurred to me that Abul's strangely selective knowledge of English had apprehended 'Twinkle Twinkle' to be the same as 'tinkle tinkle'; sometimes, a little learning is a humorous thing.

Alastair has the appearance of an angel, but not the voice. He sounds less a boy treble than a boy trouble, raucous and artless, and quite the opposite of the mannered, trilly, nasal singing popular here. Nonetheless, he finished to enthusiastic applause from those inside and outside the house. Abul's mother nodded her probative approval, then returned to her exercise of frank appraisal of us.

We spent another half hour or so, mainly exchanging comparative wonderment of our two homelands: Canada very cold, Bangladesh very hot, Canada very big, Bangladesh very small, Canada very rich, Bangladesh very poor, so few Canadians, so many Bangladeshi....

And then we rose to go. Abul attempted, and failed, to extract from us a commitment to visit his house every night we were in the village. The crowd of people parted to allow our egress; Abul's mother stood in dark consternation.

A large, self-appointed delegation, including Abul, escorted us all the way home. As we walked, Abul's manner became less genial, more concerned. He was chewing on a tough business he couldn't quite bring himself to spit out; and we knew what it was.

We bid our companions good night when we reached our front gate, but for some lengthy spell after we entered the little house, Abul could be seen standing by the gate in postures of indecisive failure. We couldn't think of a thing we could do for him.

The next day, as Tanyss was conducting a meeting of her staff, Abul's mother appeared at her office door. A young guard barred her entry, and she remonstrated sternly with him. Tanyss was able to discern snatches: "-- -- Alastair husband, Sitty wife ----" She'd come to finalize the arrangement.

Wherever we go, we are in the habit of examining local customs not for their quaintness, colour or peculiarity, but for the human intelligence that gave rise to them: in regions of overheated tropical/equatorial filth, for instance, reserving the right hand for clean functions and the left for unclean functions is more a matter of self-preservation and social benefit than laughable primitivism.

Much has been made of the issue of arranged marriage. CanLit had an inexplicable fixation with the subject for some time. It is generally treated as a strand of a woven pattern of women's oppression, but one which may be corrected in isolation, by fiat; however, if it is an element of oppression, it isn't women's, it's humanity's: we live with people whose lives present virtually no options in any other matter, for both women and men; their days, day after day, are made up of a succession of moments and chores necessary to survival to the next day; why would attitudes to marriage be placed outside the inevitabilities of every other aspect of their lives?

Tanyss and I discussed these events at length, and we concluded that if we were Sitty's parents, confronting the realistic prospects for our darling, bright, pretty little daughter, and we, by some fluke, came upon a bright, healthy, handsome Alastair who had the prospect of the best education and access to an enlightened wealthy place like Canada, we would recognize it as our iron-clad parental obligation to set Sitty on Tanyss' hip and dispatch them over to attempt the best deal with Alastair's parents. We would regard that as the most loving thing we could do for our daughter.

Alastair, of course, will make his own choice when he reaches maturity; who knows, maybe he'll choose Sitty, or someone like her. His marriage will be based not on strategic opportunity, but on his heart. In Canada, that would be adjudged his inviolable right; but from where we stand now, we see that as his extraordinary privilege.

WAHID

Wahid Wends His Way

As with all peoples, Canadians have developed certain national self-perceptions that may be exaggerated, if not mythical. One of ours is the idea of a hardy race embracing with enthusiastic participation our various winter pastimes: sure, we're a nation of hockey players, of curlers, of skaters on the Rideau Canal, everyone knows that; but how many of us actually play hockey? How many of us really understand anything about curling except the beer-drinking part? And as for the Rideau Canal, well, a puffing fifteen minutes once a year out of a sense of civic duty by obedient Ottawans is probably the norm.

Oddly, we foster these exaggerations even as we fail to acknowledge a true winter pastime into which virtually all male Canadians throw themselves with alacrity and abandon: in reality, innately, we are a nation of winter car-pushers. I'll bet that, if a careful dissection of the typical Canadian male brain were undertaken, there would be revealed the tiny alligator-clip cables that reach from the whirring-tire-on-snow-slick centre of the brain to jump start the okay-once-again-on-three centre of the brain. The Canadian baby boy's first words are "Mama" and "Straighten your wheels!"

At the first scream of a car in a snow bank, the first call of "Try rocking 'er!", all real Canadian men within earshot will quit whatever they're doing, be it birthday party or brain surgery, to eagerly launch themselves uninvited against the rear end of some stranger's car. Old men will gather to shiver on the sidewalk, shed a tear of nostalgia for their own glory days, and cry "Ma'am! Straighten your wheels!", thereby completing the circle of their days.

This intrinsic impulse is seriously stifled for the Canadian male living in South Asia, where tropical equivalent opportunities to exercise it are either rare or inappropriately acted upon. Some months ago, though, my sons and I were lucky enough to chance upon a trio of typically small, thin men struggling and failing to push a heavy SUV up a ramp into a parking garage under an apartment building. The country in which we live doesn't manufacture cars: at least, I don't believe it does; no nationally-produced cars are on the road, but given the quality of the products of its other areas of manufacture, it's just possible that it produces cars that always break down between the factory and the road. The result of this, anyway, is that any car one sees is foreign, and is on a larger scale than the diminutive national stature warrants or can easily accommodate. These poor men, not the owners but a hired driver and some starvation-wage security men, were no match for the massive vehicle, so, by instinct and without a word, my sons and I insinuated ourselves between them and began pushing.

This demonstration of alien character profoundly shocked our fellows, so much so that they ceased their efforts, leaving the full weight to fall to us, so that they could wave their hands in concerned protest. "No, no, sir!" they all cried, the reassuring structure of their social hierarchy alarmingly disrupted. However, naturally gifted amateurs that we are, we soon had the monster up the ramp, and the startled driver recovered in time to steer it into its parking stall; whereupon, he leapt from the car just as the others rushed forward, and we were all greeted with fervent hand-clasps from each of them.

I fixed steely eyes on the general direction of the smog- and concrete-obscured northern horizon. "Don't thank us," I said. "It's what we do."

68

That was one of the rare appropriately-acted-upon opportunities. The inappropriately-acted-upon opportunity arrives more frequently, and tests a Canadian strength to forbear.

To provide an example, it is necessary that I rock 'er, go in reverse a bit before trying to go forward:

When my family first came to Dhaka, we were disturbed by many of the things we saw, and still are, for that matter; we've become inured to some, but some, I hope, will shock us forever, as the alternative to being shocked is even less attractive.

One of the lesser, but real, disturbances was created by the sight of the thousands, millions of rickshaws plying these streets, adding their own colourful congesting confusion to an already completely chaotic city. Unlike the rickshaws just a bit farther east or west, these aren't pulled by wallahs on foot, but are combination rickshaw-bicycles, with wallah pedaller ahead and passenger on a narrow, shallow, utterly uncomfortable seat behind, a seat that angles forward at a degree most reminiscent of a ferris wheel seat when, at the end of the ride, an impatient carnie rocks your carriage forward to expel you. The pitch of the rickshaw seat causes a passenger to consider the precariousness of this existence with a depth and urgency that's downright philosophical, and well he might, but also causes him to sit in a poised, upright position, dignified, almost regal, if he resists the temptation to clutch desperately at the arched accordion bamboo ribs of the rickshaw's monsoon canopy. This lordly posture emphasized to me our first impression, offending both our Canadian egalitarianism and priority of self-sufficiency, that these poor wallahs were basically beasts of burden. And I swore that I would never ride in a rickshaw, much as I'd sworn at the age of fourteen that I'd never smoke cigarettes, with equal certainty and equal foregone failure.

My declaration was made before Wahid decided I was going to get to know him.

At the one grocery store that caters to the small number of diplomatic and foreign persons in this least-cosmopolitan of all major cities, there convene some of the more ambitious beggars, appealing to foreign generosity or guilt between the discouragements they receive from baton-wielding security guards. I was being followed by a number of begging children of beggars, one afternoon a few weeks after moving to our second flat in a more upper-middle class neighbourhood than our first, as I made my way home from this store; the little ones had been set on me by parental order, no doubt, but they were, like their parents, inclined to make some fun out of whatever they do at the times when they're not determined to make some misery out of whatever they do. So they bounced along with me happily enough ---- not deeply resenting the obvious fact that they were eventually to part from me empty-handed. They wouldn't leave me empty-handed, though, taking turns, when forgetting to feign some heart-rending physical disability, to place their little brown hands in my white ones ---- we were all happy enough, when a man's voiced growled behind us.

This is the most densely-populated city in the world, and one doesn't note every presence nearby; it's a foolish waste of awareness to do so; so it hadn't registered with me that our little parade had been joined. I turned to discover a small, slender, handsome man piloting a bicycle rickshaw at our pace. He wore a crisp clean shirt over a clean lungi, the gathered light cotton skirt worn by poor men. His revealed lower legs were as thin, gnarled and hard as little brown sticks. He barked

70

again in Bangla and raised his hand in a gesture of threat against the children, who, after an obligatory show of resistance, trotted away. I nodded to the man, and thanked him without conveying real gratitude, and he smiled ruefully, as if embarrassed by the demonstration of his nation's dire poverty. I proceeded on my way home.

And he kept pace with me, pedalling just behind, silently, steadily over the pitted and humped lunar surface that is a Dhaka street.

"No ride," I said, waving my hand, for some stupid reason thinking the choice was mine. "No ride."

"Excuse me, sir," he said carefully, "what is your homeland?"

"Canada."

"O, very good country, sir! Very good country!" He said it as though the credit were all mine.

"Yes," I allowed Canadianly (as opposed to a loud Americanly 'You got that right!')

"Very good people, sir, people of Canada!" he said, shifting to me a burden of proof. "Very good people! Very nicer than Americans, sir! Very smarter than Americans!" Since the U.S. invasion of Iraq, Canadians are the North Americans these Bangladeshi Muslims, who want to like everybody, are permitted to like, and they seize the chance.

"So we try to tell ourselves. I wish we proved it to ourselves more often. How many Canadians do you know?"

"I know many, sir," he lied. There weren't many to know.

"How is it that you speak English?"

"I have given many rides to people of the British High Commission."

"You learned English from giving rides to people from the British High Commission?" I asked, genuinely impressed.

"Yes, sir."

"You must be talented at languages," I said.

"Yes, sir. And very, very best rickshaw driver, sir," he said, demonstrating, for all his extensive exposure to Canadians, he was happily uncontaminated by our austere ethic that modesty is the highest virtue.

"I don't doubt you are," I said. "I, myself, am a reasonably capable walker, so I have no need for a rickshaw ride."

Not for the last time, he fixed me with a look of pitying concern for my apparent mental incapacity.

"But, sir, you are very rich."

"No, no, I am not rich."

"Yes, sir, people from Canada are very, very rich," he explained patiently.

"I'm a Canadian poet. Canada punishes its poets with poverty, as a deterrent to others who might be tempted to similar sin."

"O, ho, sir," he said, much enjoying the humour of the absurdity I was trying to put over on him. "You are very, very rich, sir."

"And you are very persistent. What's your name?"

"Wahid, sir," he said.

"Well, Wahid, at 10:30 tomorrow morning, my wife will be taking my daughter to an appointment at the American International School. Do you know where it is?"

"Yes, sir," he said, answering the sort of question I would never ask him again, as he was to reveal he held some phenomenal combination roadmap/yellow pages of Dhaka in his head, knew not only major installations like the American School, but every little shop down every nameless, narrow, confusing curlicue little pathway.

72

"That is the gate to our flat over there. Could you be there at 10:30 tomorrow?"

"O, yes sir."

I noted that he didn't wear a watch.

It was only later that it occurred to me that Wahid's internal encyclopaedia of all things Dhakan probably contained an entry on the annual tuition cost of the American International School, which would approximate maybe twenty-years' income for an industrious rickshaw wallah, and that any subsequent attempt to convince him that we would never have been able to afford the tuition from our own resources, and that we weren't wealthy, was about as useful as snowshoes.

It turned out that Tanyss was unavoidably otherwise occupied the next morning, and it was necessary for me to go with Grace to the school, so my determination not to ride in a rickshaw lasted a mere three months.

Wahid showed up at 10:30 on the dot.

He helped Grace up into the little seat, and I climbed up beside her. I would have felt more confident perched on a spice rack.

"We wish to go to the American School," I said.

"Yes, sir," Wahid said, hopping up and straining on the pedals to get us going. "In Bangla, 'Ami American School jaboo.'"

"Really."

"You say, sir. Ami American School jaboo," he instructed as we lurched into the turbulent flow of the main road.

"I can't say 'jaboo'," I protested, saying 'jaboo'.

"Why not, sir?"

"Because it's undignified," I said, pausing to clutch desperately at the arched accordion bamboo ribs of the rickshaw's monsoon canopy.

His rickshaw was sure rickety, rusty and ragged. The narrow board under our feet was cracked and rotting, and I saw that Wahid's bike seat was broken along the middle, with a stiff edge sticking up. It must have been most uncomfortable.

As we went into the international area of the city, he pointed out the various embassies and high commissions like a tour guide. He delivered us safely at the school, and I asked that he return to take us home in two hours.

He was waiting for us then.

On our way home, we passed through the circle of the local downscale, everyone-else's market, a jumble of carts, stalls, booths, and tiny shops, of ranks of tailors hunched over sidewalk sewing machines, of meat markets where that chunk of buffalo was standing on four legs five minutes ago, of heaped chickens, odious orange deep-fried foods, piles of cheap jersey clothing, precarious mountains of produce with the sellers sitting at the pinnacles like swamis with woven baskets on long poles to take your taka, of swirling stinks and cacophonous haggling. I thought we'd stop and help out our housekeeper/cook, Ratan, by doing the daily shopping.

For some reason, the fishmongers seem to be the most aggressive, and Grace and I were, as always, pursued throughout the pathways of the market by teenaged boys carrying still-startled fish (perhaps they were additionally surprised to be called salmon), loudly impressing upon us that such bargains would not arise again in our lifetimes. Some boys argued with us vehemently that we did so need new aluminum cooking

74

pots and palm floor mats. Grace or Tanyss were better to shop with than one of my sons, as the pressing hawkers yielded us an extra six inches space in deference to a female.

When we'd bought our groceries, which we did quite efficiently, taking only six or seven times as long as one would reasonably expect, we boarded Wahid's rattletrap and rode home. Ratan and Beauty, presumably summoned by the houseboys or guards of the ground-level parking garage, met us to take the groceries, including the little paper bag of inevitably broken eggs, over which Ratan could have the pleasure of mildly tsk-tsking: his mastery of their safe transport I'll never understand.

I asked Wahid what we owed him.

"Sir, a Bangladeshi I would charge one hundred taka, sir."

"Yes? And so?"

"A foreigner, two hundred taka, sir."

Ratan and Beauty, both of whom are very protective of us, were aghast and angered. Ratan chided him severely in Bangla, and Beauty tossed in her one-taka's-worth (= 2 cents), too. Wahid answered back, briefly, and shrugged. I paid him the two hundred, even as Ratan and Beauty shook their heads in emphatic disagreement. I actually quite appreciated his quirky honesty, little knowing that this was to be but the first exercise of a perpetual campaign to separate us from our vast wealth.

The next day, at ten-thirty, the in-house telephone rang, and in a moment Ratan was tapping at my bedroom/office door.

"Sorry for disturb, sir. Wahid is waiting downstairs."

"He is? What does he want?"

"For ride, sir."

I suggested that Ratan use the ride to go to the market. He seemed somewhat reluctant, but agreed.

It became the daily thing, and soon enough I faced facts and negotiated a monthly amount for Wahid to take Ratan or Beauty to the market once a day, and to take Tanyss and me to a restaurant every Saturday evening.

On those Saturday evenings, we got to know Wahid better. We learned that he was married with two young children, that they lived in one room in a slum some miles away. Once we asked him what his ambition was for his life, and he answered without hesitation:

"For people to know me as a great man, to be honoured."

That aspiration mightn't go over too well voiced aloud in, say, a Canadian living room on a Saturday night, but riding through a Saturday night milling crowd of lives treated as no more than bricks in somebody else's haphazard, unapproved, code-noncompliant building project, his individualistic ambition seemed permissible, if unlikely.

Another time, he told us about a calamitous raise in the rental rate for his rickshaw.

"You mean you rent this torturous piece of rubbish? How much do you pay?"

He told us that he'd been paying seventy taka per day, in advance, but the rate was suddenly increased to a hundred. We asked him why he didn't buy his own rickshaw, and he held up his hand, rubbing his fingers and thumb together in the international signal of what so many of us don't have enough of. He explained that, until he'd gotten his regular duty with us, he'd been hard pressed to make back the seventy taka many days, and what a hardship the increase would impose.

"I don't suppose the increase would result in a replacement bicycle seat," I said.

"No, sir."

"How much would a rickshaw cost?" Tanyss asked.

He answered with suspicious readiness: eighty hundred taka. For under three month's rental, he could have his own, but he was never able to accumulate that amount at one time. He fell silent after telling us, probably to allow a period of quiet reflection on the inequities of life.

Tanyss and I talked things over during dinner, and, as Wahid rode us home, we told him we'd lend him the money for his own rickshaw. He was very pleased, if not as apparently surprised as we might have liked.

We brought him up to our flat to delineate the terms of repayment, with which he agreed wholeheartedly and without any intention of fulfilling. Our idea that he set up as an independent businessman was a complete non-starter with him. He is a very proud man, much prouder than most rickshaw wallahs feel they have the luxury to be, but he was quite satisfied, it turned out, that he could be his own man enough within the protection and advantages of our employ.

Our Canadian sensibilities led us astray, too, when we expected the matter of obtaining a rickshaw would be accomplished in a day or two. We failed to consider the south Asian credo that if something's worth doing, it's worth doing elaborately decorated; Wahid found a rickshaw to buy smartly enough, but it was then weeks in the preparation; that it was only fifty-percent over budget Wahid treated as much a happy surprise as fifty percent under would have been to me.

One day, however, I received an urgent call from the houseboys downstairs that I must come down. When I got there, I found a small crowd of people gathered outside the gate, and there, in the centre of the admiring circle, was Wahid with his rickshaw. And what a rickshaw: every square inch was painted with some design. Brass balls and plastic streamers sprouted from every supporting surface. On its back panels were depictions of the Bangladeshi and Canadian flags, and laminated portraits of Grace and Alastair with their names beneath. My name was written across one, and in a swirling design, the name Md. Wahid Miah, the proud wallah, and the important message 'PRIVET RISAKA'; and on its mud guard below, a dramatic scene from some Bollywood film. Each bamboo rib of the canopy carried curlicues of colour; exotic birds and flowers festooned every free space; the passenger seat was of bright yellow plastic with a stylized geometric flower on the lower section, and another dramatic set of heroic/villainous Bollywood portraits on the back rest; and just below the seat, across a panel in large letters 'WELCOME'. It was dazzling.

The excited houseboys took turns taking it for little spins, after ascertaining that I didn't feel the need to first. The air was celebrative; I shook Wahid's hand and congratulated him; then he directed my attention to a young man hanging back just outside the circle, and explained that this was the craftsman responsible for the work of wonder, so I shook his hand, too, and then Wahid let me know that the young man was disappointed that my hand had held nothing but his.

"Sir, buksis," Wahid said patiently.

"Buksis? But I've just paid him thousands and thousands of taka," I protested.

"Yes, sir, but happiness, sir."

"Whose happiness?"

"Your happiness, sir, show happiness."

"But if I give him buksis, I won't have any happiness."

"Oh ho, sir," Wahid laughed. "Very funny, sir."

I can't remember how much buksis we settled on, but the happiness seemed to be mainly Wahid's.

One of Tanyss' colleagues hired him for a daily run, as well. It would seem that Wahid was sitting pretty, or at least pretty comfortably, with his plush new seat. However, within days he was quietly escalating his campaign against our pockets.

His licence was expensive. I don't know if the amount included buksis, but there's no reason why it wouldn't. Then there was the cost of securing the rickshaw at night within a closed compound, which possibly doubled as protection graft. Then there was the matter of the bell. Wallahs of lesser rickshaws found it workable just to shout at other wallahs or drivers or pedestrians who impeded them, but it would no longer do for Wahid. A very fine electronic bell was had for a mere four hundred taka. It sounded like a car theft alarm, and I could only hope others in our path found it as insufferable as I did. Alas, then there was the ongoing need for its batteries.

Electric turn signals mounted on the back became absolutely essential, even though generally the streets were so jammed, no one behind us would actually be able to see them. Wahid presented the bill after their installation. Unfortunately, they chirped in a most irksome way. Our rickshaw came to sound like a stolen pet-store delivery van, became a significant contributor to Dhaka's grievous noise pollution.

Sometimes he would fail to take us where we wished to go, but would slowly trace a route around it, until we noticed and asked him what was wrong, at which time, as we'd forced him, he would reluctantly reveal his latest urgent requirement:

"Sir, our rickshaw is better than all others?"

"So it seems."

"My raincoat isn't better than all others. It is just ordinary, sir."

"It works, doesn't it? It keeps you dry."

"It is not suitable, sir."

"I see. How much does a suitable coat cost?"

"Seven hundred fifty only, sir."

Other times his ploy was more inventive, if not more direct, such as:

"Sir, other wallahs are asking me, 'When is your sir buying you your mobile phone?' I laugh at them, sir, laugh at them. I tell them 'My sir will be buying me my mobile very, very soon, in his good time.' And then we'll laugh at them together, won't we, sir?"

"Why do you need a mobile, Wahid?"

"To come at once when you need me, sir."

As a matter of fact, we'd soon discovered that both Wahid and we were well known within the rickshaw brotherhood, and all we had to do was call out 'Wahid' to a passing wallah, and within half an hour Wahid would be waiting at our gate. If I'd pointed this out to him, though, I'm sure he would have thereafter proven the method's unreliability.

Incessantly, he complained that he needed a raise in his wage, just to make ends meet.

One day, I asked why, with his situation apparently so improved, he still couldn't cope.

"I don't understand. You've got two regular routes that pay you something, you've got your own rickshaw for which you've obviously decided you won't make any payments, after all, and you've got most of every day to earn extra money. I know you aren't going to get rich, but why are you no better off than you were?"

He put up his hands and shook his head, but in another moment I was to get a partial answer. Across the road from where we were, there stood a Bangladeshi businessman who was motioning to Wahid to come to him.

"There's a fare for you," I said. "You'd better go and get him."

At first, he pretended not to hear me. When I repeated myself, he gave his head a tiny shake and looked away.

"Wahid, why are you ignoring a chance to get more money?"

"Sir, he's 'deshi," he said simply.

So Wahid the proud had been elevated to a new status, where he pedalled for foreigners only. No doubt he'd boasted such with the other wallahs.

"You know," I said, "my family associates every day with poor 'deshis, including a poor 'deshi rickshaw wallah. We've always found them to be plenty good enough for us."

He looked at me.

"I don't think this is the path to greatness, my friend," I said.

Rickshaw wallahs are treated as little better than vermin by many here in Dhaka, even though they perform a useful service, so it's understandable that Wahid would wish to create a new, higher classification for himself. City police, in particular, have an apparent blanket hatred of rickshaw wallahs, and seem to set up impromptu restricted areas just for the chance to crack wallahs' heads and puncture rickshaw tires. When we started giving evening classes in the slums, and so added two more rides a day to Wahid's workload (so he got his raise after all, of course, of course), we regularly came upon newly erected barbed-wire barriers and baton-happy police. The first time an officer set in to crown Wahid, I raised my hand in the path of his baton.

"This man is a member of my household," I said. "I shall treat any abuse of him as a personal offence against me."

I don't know how much English the policeman had, but he was able to deduce enough to revise his intentions and withdraw.

From then on, I believe, Wahid deliberately sought out restricted routes, just so he could smugly refer the police to my pretence of authority.

"Canada, private rickshaw," he would say, gesturing back to me.

It never failed.

He suggested to me once that it was under our aegis, too, that he was permitted to operate his rickshaw free of retribution from his former rickshaw renter.

As being our employee was all by his design, not ours, we hadn't any formal protocols of his employment. In theory, he answers to Ratan, a relationship that is always strained, as Ratan, as honest and upright as can be, continues to scorn Wahid as a conniving manipulator of our good will. Otherwise, the conditions are pretty much improvised. Such as:

"Sir, I must take two weeks away starting tomorrow."

"You must?"

"Yes, sir. We must go to my wife's village. Her father has died."

"Her father?"

"Yes, sir."

"Wahid, you have just the one wife, I believe. Mahamuda?"

"Yes, sir. One wife. Mahamuda."

"So that would be the same father who died two months ago. I suppose he never fully recovered from the first time he died."

"No, sir."

After some months with us, Wahid invited Tanyss and me to his house for lunch. On the agreed day, he picked us up, but had to stop en route in the international area; he had consulted with a friend who worked as a peon in the home of a British diplomat about the proper entertainment we should be offered, and was told that cucumber sandwiches were what foreigners loved; the whole concept of cucumber sandwiches defied Mahamuda's comprehension, so the helpful peon had agreed to make them, and it was these we stopped to pick up, one little, crust-trimmed sandwich apiece.

He stopped the rickshaw at the edge of his slum, and then led us through a labyrinth of passageways between tiny, sandy concrete boxes, out of the doors of which people spilled to look at us.

Eventually, we reached his own house, one small room in which waited Mahamuda, a shy but very pleasant person, most welcoming, their little daughter, Sharmin, who seemed to be about four years old, although neither of her parents could tell us for sure, and on the one bed, their naked baby boy, Alamgir.

Wahid bade us sit in the place of honour, on the edge of the bed, and then excused himself to fetch his neighbour, a bright young man whose facility in English had landed him a low job at the British High Commission. His name was Rashid, and he was very pleasant company. His talents, I'm sure, far outstripped his duties at the BHC, but, for this neighbourhood, he had high prestige, hence his invitation to visit with us. Still, he didn't rate a cucumber sandwich.

Wahid disappeared again to fetch from somewhere a bottle of the ubiquitous 'Ten Up' (as Gabriel says, like Seven Up, but better by a full three), which he'd managed to have chilled especially for us. Bangladeshis abhor cold drinks.

As we'd expected, Wahid's little house was drab and spare, with nothing but the most basic essentials to be seen on the little shelf; it was small wonder he was so keen on all the bells and whistles on his rickshaw.

Typically, a crowd of curious people had gathered at, and in, the doorway. One of the people leaning in through the door was a beautiful girl of ten or eleven who watched me solemnly. I found something about her so arresting, my eyes kept returning to her, and her observation was steady.

Eventually, I asked Wahid if she were a member of his family.

"Is Bisli, sir, wife sister daughter."

"So your niece?"

"Yes, sir, my niece. Her father died yesterday."

Wahid, of course, lies often, but he's an honest man at heart, and when he lies he has the decency to tell you so with a subtle curl of the lip, a very small crinkle at the corner of his eye. I searched his face and found no trace.

I looked back at Bisli, regarded her a long time.

Then she withdrew from the doorway, but she returned in just a few minutes, dared to venture right into the room, to stand beside me. She held something behind her, which, after a slight pause, she brought forth for me to see. It was her school exercise book.

I took it from her and leafed through it. The level of work seemed to me to be at about Grade One, by Canadian standards, but it was very neat and carefully done.

I knew why it was necessary for her to show me what a good girl she was.

"Bisli, what is your class?"

She thought a moment for the English.

"Class Four," she said.

In nearly five years, her teachers hadn't made any more of her abilities than that. One obscure but significant statistic regarding education in Bangladesh is that it ranks worst for what is called 'teacher contact time', the amount of time per day the pupils actually have the benefit of their teacher, at one and a half hours. A Canadian pupil usually gets five. It's also understood that many teachers deliberately do a poor job of teaching in the mornings so that parents will have to hire them as tutors in the afternoon, a result of the paltry pay a teacher earns.

"Will Bisli be allowed to continue in school, Wahid?" Tanyss asked.

"Not now, madam. No money now."

She needn't have asked. There's no margin for error in those places, and the thread that had lifted Bisli slightly above other children, a fortunate father's little income, was gossamer. Whatever slender hope she'd had for her life before, her future was as much laid out as her father; without education and from an impoverished, fatherless family, she would be married within the next couple of years, to keep her dowry low, to a boy without the personal prospects for his parents to negotiate his way into a more advantageous family; maybe if she were lucky/unlucky she might chance into a slave-wage job in a sweat-shop garment factory, or maybe such a beautiful girl would find her way leading into prostitution, servicing Korean business moguls or doped diplobrat sons of ambassadors. Her family's ambitions for her, and what nature had obviously conferred upon her, were now worth absolutely nothing.

I gave her notebook back to her.

"Very good work, Bisli," I said.

She smiled.

Tanyss and I ate one half of a cucumber sandwich each pro forma, and drank a little glass of Ten Up, and after letting a long parade peer through the doorway at us as we played with Alamgir and chatted, we drew the visit to a conclusion.

As Wahid pedalled us home, he was unusually quiet. Either he was thinking deeply of something, or he was hoping we were.

I cracked.

"Wahid, we'll raise your wage enough for you to hire a tutor for Bisli and Sharmin."

"Yes, sir. Thank you, sir."

"A tutor, mind you, not some underachieving school. And we'll want to see that the tutor's earning his money."

"Yes, sir. That will be very good, sir."

"It's not very good, Wahid, and it's no real solution," I said. "What about all the other beautiful children in the same situation whom we didn't happen to meet today?"

With those words, it seems, I unintentionally set a bug in Wahid's ear, and it grew in his mind into what he beheld as a glorious butterfly.

Within a few days, he reported to us that he'd organized a number of his neighbours into hiring a tutor jointly, to defray the cost to all. We congratulated him on his atypical concern for my economy.

He wasn't done, however. In hindsight, I'll guess that his organizational efforts had won him the approbation of his neighbours, and at no cost to himself, and, being a quick study and sharp opportunist, he began to think on a larger scale.

I don't remember any in particular, but I suppose he'd had the chance to absorb discussions between

86

Tanyss and me about the charitable schools we were operating for children in those days, even as we were in the process of concluding that we needed a more efficient approach to the huge problem; or, perhaps, Ratan had spoken to him about our schools. At any rate, in another couple of weeks, Wahid asked if Tanyss and I would come to his slum to confer with some parents there about the creation of a school. We said that we'd certainly be willing to talk with them, and it was arranged that Wahid would take us that following Saturday afternoon.

Our expectation, as Wahid rode us to his slum that afternoon, was that we'd meet with a handful of neighbours and talk about whatever they had in mind, give them the benefit of our advice, shake hands, wish them well, offer to advise them at any time, and then go home. I'll accept that we probably should have known better than that, given how altogether too normal and rational that would have been, but I maintain that even our experience of the unexpected couldn't have prepared us for into what we were delivered.

I remember noting how the narrow streets of the slum seemed awfully empty of their usual crowds, but this curiosity didn't trip the alarm bell. It was when we came around a curve to find a very large, brightly-coloured sort of open-sided tent erected upon a rubble-strewn open patch (probably where city bulldozers had levelled a section of the illegal slum, an exercise undertaken sporadically, possibly as a result of a palm going uncrossed) that I came to sense something seriously amiss. At the same time that it became obvious that within the tent were most of the number missing from the streets, it became clear that it was where Wahid was steering us.

"Um, Wahid...," I said.

"Yes, sir, everything is ready, sir."

"What everything?"

"Everything, everything, sir. We are all ready."

There were hundreds under the canopy, babies, children, men and women, old men and old women.

Wahid leapt off his rickshaw and smiled happily.

"This is rather more than we...." I began.

"Good, sir, very good. So many."

He led us through the watchful assembly to the front of the tent. There were three plastic stools set there. Children touched our arms as we passed through. When we reached the stools, Wahid motioned for us to sit, and then sat on the third stool himself. The front ranks of the crowd squatted down in the dirt and chunks of sandy concrete.

Rashid, the young man who works at the British High Commission, came forward and began a speech. Everyone listened attentively. When he mentioned Mr. Wahid ---- not Wahid, but Mr. Wahid ---- there was a spontaneous outburst of applause. Wahid rose to acknowledge it, smiling and waving in a general way. Rashid went on to mention Mr. Wahid several times, and each time the applause was forthcoming, and each time Wahid stood to accept it.

His smile was serene, nearly saintly.

In the audience, his shy wife stood beaming, baby boy in her arms, happy daughter by her side.

One of the reasons, just one of the reasons, that Tanyss and I love these people is because, like us, they have absolutely no idea what's impossible.

Rashid concluded by introducing Mr. Wahid for his own speech, and Wahid stood and introduced the ten men of the school committee (!), each of whom stood to applause. Then Wahid held aloft the list of three hundred families that had already signed up for the free school (!!). Then he, in a peripheral way, mentioned his Madam and Sir who would operate it, before returning to clarify and expand upon his own pivotal position in the entire matter.

At the end of his speech, he stood smiling and waving to the hundreds pouring out their appreciation. He was basking in the fulfilment of his life's ambition: he was being seen as a great man; he was being honoured.

Just then would have been the very time for me to teach Wahid something about the Canadian virtue, not of modesty, but of modesty-enforcement, to enact the Canadian's trusted tradition of taking him down a peg or two, for his own good, to tell the eager, hopeful people that Tanyss and I hadn't agreed to opening a school, hadn't even been asked about it, and that Wahid and his committee were naught but presumptuous self-aggrandizers making fools of themselves and their neighbours.

But I guess I, negligently, failed to consider his own good. When Rashid called upon me to speak and provided translation, I congratulated Wahid on his extraordinary feat of organization, congratulated his committee members on their contribution, and congratulated all the parents who had demonstrated their own commitment to their children's education. The fact is, I didn't want to be the one to tell them what's impossible, and I wanted to see Wahid being a great man a while longer. Tanyss understood, too, without a word between us.

After the meeting, accompanied by two dozen skinny little darlings trying to hold our hands at once, Tanyss and I were conducted to a six-storey apartment building at the edge of the slum. Wahid explained that there was an important man we must meet.

The important man, it turned out, was the landlord of some chunks of the slum; it seemed he was unavailable to meet with us, and we were received by his eldest son, instead, a good-looking twenty-three year old with a relaxed, confident manner. The committee had come with us, but only Wahid was permitted to enter with us. We were seated on garishly ornate furniture.

The young man sat down and, speaking only to me, stated that if we were to find a room or group of rooms for the school, it would be necessary to negotiate rental through his family.

He annoyed me. I wondered if his father was also the rickshaw renter.

"If we were to donate a charitable school to the neighbourhood from which you profit, we would expect you to donate premises," I said.

He smiled slightly, and said, "We should speak about it after entertainment." By entertainment, he meant refreshment.

"I'm sorry, we haven't time for entertainment," I said.

Scales fell over his eyes, and he put his head to one side, and raised the palms of his hands.

"My father's house," he said, warning me of the offence I was about to give.

"Your father doesn't see fit to welcome us."

I glanced at Wahid. He was hunched forward in his seat, looking somewhat less great.

The son sized me up a moment, and then gave a little signal to someone outside the doorway.

In a minute, an old woman brought in a tray of small glasses of Ten Up and some milk biscuits, and she was soon followed by a stout middle-aged man.

"My father," said the young man by way of introduction.

The father at least had the courtesy to acknowledge Tanyss.

As we sipped, I reiterated what would, conjecturally, be our position toward rent.

"We will work something out," the father assured us warmly.

I thought that unlikely, and I was right. We received word from him some time later that what he could work out was to charge us about four times what he normally would for a room.

As we were going home, the great man pedalling in front of us was silent.

"He's taking us the long way home," Tanyss noted.

We knew what that meant.

"Wahid, how much, and what's it for?"

"Fifteen-hundred taka, sir. Rental charge for tent."

It took about four days for the school committee to factionalize. Wahid had reason to believe that a certain Jamal had only joined the committee to obtain from us a recommendation for a job at the Canadian High Commission for which he was clearly unqualified. Wahid moved for his ouster; Jamal responded by proposing a bylaw requiring all committee members to be literate, which would have had the effect of leaving him as a committee of one. A fatal stalemate ensued.

The ruction had no bearing on us. Touching though the public assembly had been, Tanyss and I soon decided that we had to use our scant resources more effectively. Our intention is that, when our means allow, we'll set up one of our more sustainable schools for mothers in that slum, so they can become the teachers of their children; Wahid's idea of a supervising committee of men won't be incorporated, of course ---- anyway, a classroom full of women is its own committee ---- but if Wahid wishes to claim credit for its genesis, that will be fine with us.

I don't know if the failure of the children's school to materialize so far has diminished Wahid's new stature. If so, I've no doubt it will be only temporarily, for somehow he came to construe something that landlord will never understand in a month of Fridays, that, for the poor man, the true path to greatness and honour lies not through straining to elevate himself above and apart from those around him, but through service to them. Wahid is a smart fellow, and he's not about to forget what he's learned. And if there's as much ego as ethic in his motivation, well, ego more often manifests itself in less worthy ways; the good works will still be done, and Wahid's greatness and honour will be assured.

Within the world of rickshaw wallahs, he's already great, maybe the best, as he claimed; he's safe, knowledgeable, intuitive, mindful of our comfort and strikes the right balance of assertion and deference; he's head and shoulder above most other wallahs, who are none of those things. As for his schemes against our savings account, I find I'm more forgiving than Ratan: I've met the three sweetest of his motivating factors, and he always plays by rules we both understand.

And that brings us to the inappropriately-acted-upon opportunities to exercise the Canadian impulse: the roads in Dhaka are so uneven, so unfortunately topographic, Wahid occasionally comes upon a hump or hillock over which his pin legs won't power his rickshaw. When that happens, he slides smoothly and swiftly from his seat to push the rickshaw over the obstacle, and, invariably, Azien, Gabriel or I will immediately, impulsively long to hop down with him and help him push; of course, to hop off would obviate the necessity to hop off, but, more importantly, Wahid wouldn't see it as an assistance, but as an insult to his professional ability, a denial of his convoluted and uplifted path to greatness.

Rohima to the Rescue

ROHIMA

Rohima to the Rescue

It's said that travel is broadening. With the quality of airline food, I'm usually a bit thinner after travelling, even after all the sitting; but living in a place that, in many ways, is as unlike Canada as can be has greatly widened our range of what we see as normal. By normal, I don't mean natural, and I certainly don't mean acceptable; dreadful poverty is normal here, it's normal that disease and disfigurement are displayed before the mosques on Fridays, it's normal that police baton rickshaw wallahs and guards baton beggars, that people die of typhoid in the slums, that monga, seasonal starvation, strikes the northern agricultural workers in the winter, etc., etc., all normal, all unnatural, all unacceptable.

Some things, however, still strike us as very peculiar. One of them is this story of Rabeya and Rohima:

There was in Dhaka a poor woman named Fatima, a mother of two sons and two daughters, and she was extraordinarily determined and domineering, lacking the generosity that allows cooperation and the courage that enables exploration to see where events might lead of a volition other than her own; she was rigid and demanding, and scheming and selfish. She bullied her husband and cowed her children, and beat them with a stick both in fury and by calculation.

They lived in a very poor neighbourhood, in a tiny soft concrete row-house in a small complex of identical houses arranged in a series of ranks separated by narrow dirt walkways in which fur-bare curs curled in sleep, dirty cats, as angular as starving cows, prowled for rats, and faint-hope hens pecked, and happier children played with wooden tops set spinning in the dirt by lengths of jute twine, or invented games with broken bits of whatever gleaned from the nearest garbage heap.

Parents in such a circumstance are behoved to consider ways to improve their situation, but most see their children as the reasons for improvement, not commodities to be brokered for it.

Not unusually, Fatima's children were afforded no education, but unlike most other parents there, the absence of a child's opportunity wasn't a cause of this mother's sorrow, which seemed motivated entirely by her longing for the material items she didn't have.

People in those cramped neighbourhoods live in each others' laps. Close interaction is inescapable. As she was so hot and ruthless in attack --- always masked as defence or appropriate retribution for some grievance --- her milder-mannered neighbours found it easiest to acquiesce in the face of her tempers and vendettas, and, as weak characters find the need and means to do, she was able to exact a measure of rueful obedience from them. She established herself as something of a local thug.

As might have been predicted, under her domestic tyranny, Fatima's faint-heart hen-pecked husband did little to distinguish himself, and none of her first three children showed anything worth commenting on. Fatima's youngest, however, a daughter named Rabeya, was a lovely child, a blossom of life's surpassing determination to renew itself wherever it may, and a demonstration that where there is life, there is hope. Her air was as fragrant as her mother's was acrid. As much as people feared Fatima, they cared for Rabeya.

Early marriage is a serious social problem here, but a resort of most poor parents of girls; to blame is a peculiar traditional dowry system wherein the bride's family must pay the groom, or his family, a negotiated amount, and the amount rises with the age of the bride. The result is babies having babies, an unnatural situation fraught with ongoing ills: babies don't produce good babies. I came to know a sweet girl surely no older than 14 who begged everyday on the streets, dressed in tatters, her chronically sickly toddler by her side and her sickly infant in her little arms.

I've never understood how it could have come to be that the girl's family pays the dowry, anyway. Any healthy society recognizes that the good young women are its treasures. Tanyss and I used to teach, in our schools in remote aboriginal communities in Canada, about the common First Nations traditions where, by one means or another according to the custom of each tribe, a prospective groom was required to prove his worthiness and capabilities to the bride's family; that makes sense.

When Rabeya reached the age of fourteen, Fatima gave her in marriage to a boy named Biplob.

The thinking behind arranged marriages here doesn't dismiss love entirely, it just doesn't credit it as a reliable predictor of marital success; it's expected that, if the parents are prudent and practical in their considerations, and the bride and groom are dutiful to each other, the marriage will succeed, and love will naturally develop.

We may deduce from her subsequent actions that Fatima was being less practical than tactical in arranging Rabeya's early marriage to Biplob.

Still, Rabeya was a dutiful daughter, and she settled into becoming a dutiful young wife to Biplob, who had the sense to recognize that he was a very fortunate young husband. As is normal, she left her father's house and went to live with Biplob's family. Her predictable future would not strike the progressive mind as rich with potential for fulfilment; being very poor and raising children to be very poor in one's place is not repaying life's investment, and can't, by the most sympathetic assessment, be regarded as answering even function, let alone purpose, but the underdeveloped mind dwells with little context around the moment; the past is merely a collection of those moments, and the future an imprecise, illogical anticipation of more moments; that she was, in the immediate, relieved of her mother's fiery domination and attached to an agreeable boy encouraged her cheerful nature.

It isn't known what worm began to chew in Fatima's mind; perhaps she missed her daughter's help in the little household, resented that Rabeya spent her days in assistance to her mother-in-law; maybe Biplob didn't show the initiative she'd hoped would carry her out of poverty along with Rabeya; perhaps she saw other mothers making more advantageous matches and was envious. Whatever the reason, she began to attempt to sow discord between the young couple by extravagant criticism and lies of misdeeds.

Her campaign didn't work. Rabeya, being a tender girl, had grown to love Biplob, and Biplob, being a boy with eyes in his head and a heart in his chest, had quickly grown to love her in return.

Their devotion to one another maddened Fatima. Whatever might have motivated her at first was replaced by a simple fury that she'd failed to force her will upon them. In time, she devised a crude and wicked plot.

With the justification of some trumped-up transgression, she demanded, and gained, the assistance of her own family and of some of her neighbours. She sent for the young couple, and when they came to her house, they were seized.

Biplob was locked in one room, and Rabeya was locked into another very small dark room, little more than a closet.

Fatima presented Biplob with a declaration of divorce and ordered him to sign it. He refused, declaring instead his love for Rabeya. From her little cell, Rabeya pled with her mother, and called out her love for Biplob.

They beat Biplob. Frantic Rabeya begged her mother for a mercy that found no space within that stunted maternal heart.

Biplob was a nice young fellow, but he wasn't made of the sternest Spartan stoicism, and after a couple of days, and with sufficient savage beating, he signed the paper and staggered away. Police in Dhaka had never arrived at any "To Serve and Protect" platitudes, and their fundamental function, the receiving of hefty bribes to serve and protect the interests of the very few wealthy against the needs of the very many poor, was well understood. Intimidated by Fatima's fierce reputation and the obedience of her local coterie now reinforced by shared complicity, and without any money for recourse through the law, Biplob's family did nothing, and Rabeya was never to see her young man again.

She proved to be far more steadfast, and Spartan scarcely describes what she undertook. Whatever advantage Fatima had hoped to gain, she didn't get it. Held in the little house, Rabeya fell into heartbroken desolation, and for days she wailed and implored her impotent father and pitiless mother; Fatima's stick, frequently applied, raised the volume of the girl's lamentations along with the welts, but for the first time Fatima faced a resolve as rigid as her own; perhaps it was her unwitting gift to her daughter. At any rate, the girl's grief gradually gave way to a programme of depressive non-compliance.

When her crying stopped, she fell completely silent, and nothing would induce her to speak. She refused to do the chores her mother assigned her, frustrating brutal coercion. Fatima's final threat to withhold food was obviated by Rabeya's refusal to eat, and when her mother had then to command her to eat, the girl only ate erratic handfuls, and never at family meals. She wasn't content to settle into that, however, and escalated her defiance by refusing to bathe. Stringent personal cleanliness is regarded as a fundamental virtue in this land of fetid tropical incubation, and its neglect as depravity.

Whatever her mother might wish, Rabeya anticipated and refused. By the time Rabeya refused to clothe herself, Fatima was beside herself, frantic at the dishonour her daughter was bringing her, and terrified by her apparent insanity.

Mother and father enclosed their daughter back in the dark little cell, and there they kept her very badly, naked and unwashed and barely fed, for the next fourteen years.

A society where life seems to be grasped only by the fingertips, where change is almost synonymous with disaster, where there is so little margin for error, dreams of the phantom control, and dreams that a path to control begins with obedience to a chain of authority, which most certainly includes a daughter's obedience to parental authority. A child's rebellion frightens everyone in those underdeveloped echelons; individualism is a progressive concept of which most of them are incapable.

In the early days of Rabeya's imprisonment, certain neighbours protested on her behalf, but they were trespassing against the principle of parental authority, and then they were subjected to Fatima's vehement invective and threats of vengeance against their interference, and all withdrew, unhappily convinced they'd done all they could.

One of the people to protest was a woman named Rohima, and, although she could think of nothing more to do for Rabeya, she alone wasn't satisfied she'd done all that was possible.

Rohima was of that neighbourhood, but she wasn't to remain there, precisely. Her husband had initiative that poor Biplob had lacked, and he and Rohima and their little daughters were on their way to a higher stratum of the hierarchy. By hard work and ability, they built a small but viable car rental business. Even after they were able to buy a flat in a lower middle-class building on the outskirt of the poor neighbourhood, Rohima was troubled by the cruel fate of tragic Rabeya.

Now it is necessary to draw a line of our own history to converge with that of Rabeya and Rohima.

When our family came to Bangladesh, it was under the auspices of an international agency that wanted Tanyss to find ways to bring improvements to the country's deficient standards of education. This wasn't an easy task, as the government of the day was chary of education, knowing that their best hopes were with an uneducated, uninformed electorate given to emotion more than reason; in other words, it was not dissimilar to two North American governments of the day.

Almost all the schools here are what Canadians would call private schools, of a range of costs and quality from a majority that are relatively cheap and bad to a very few that are extremely expensive and fairly good. Tanyss and I quite soon realized that there was a desperate problem in that millions of families couldn't afford to educate their children at all, and that they would

100

be perpetually subject to the predations of poverty and ignorance.

Our family's first experiments in addressing this intolerable problem were the creation of a few free schools for very poor children. While we really enjoyed this direct approach, as the children were as keen and lovable as could be, it soon became obvious to us that it wasn't adequately sustainable, and was, of course, just a spit in the ocean, given the scope of the problem. I once made the mistake of starting to calculate roughly by what fantastic multiples the birth rate would outstrip our very best hopes of opening new schools. Also, the violent political disruptions and murderous religious extremists of that time were interfering with our ability to get to our far-flung schools.

Tanyss and I were chewing over this tough problem, sitting in one of our village schools, when fate intervened, perhaps. It has become part of the lore and legend of Amarok Society in BD that a higher power has propelled its progress at its continuous critical moments; either that, or our operations here have encountered a most remarkable series of coincidences; Tanyss and I tend toward the destiny explanation, a drill-sergeant sort of destiny determined that we do more and more work at greater and greater personal cost. Destiny-driven enterprises require accompanying legend, and our BD family has not been remiss in recording and repeating its tales.

Outside the barred window of the village school in which we sat, little more than a tin shed, really, two local young women began a very vociferous argument, so loudly that it prevented our discussion. We recognized them as mothers of two of our sweet little pupils. After a quarter hour of bitter recrimination, the two women were showing no sign of slowing down; a husband of one took his wife by the arm and tried to lead her away, and the husband of the other woman attempted to reason with her, but they'd have none of it. The first wife whipped her arm away and launched new assaults, and the other pushed her husband aside and parried and thrust, so to speak, or so to scream, actually. It was another half hour before the husbands managed to manoeuvre their fuming wives away from each other. In the echoes to follow, I said to Tanyss, "Those women don't have enough to do." From that, we very soon realized that, in our discussion of the resources that might be available to us, we'd been overlooking a vast, untapped, self-renewing resource of incalculable value.

We began to discuss with large agencies the idea of teaching mothers to become teachers of their own and their neighbours' children. The usual reaction was that it was a brilliant idea of startling innovation, and that they wouldn't touch it with a ten-mile pole; in the first place, they couldn't get access to the lowest slums we were talking about, environs of those elusive bottom-layer children they scratch their heads about how to reach, and in the second place, the women of that caste were in disarray and unmanageable, and, thirdly, illiterate adults of a lineage of illiteracy weren't teachable to the extent that they could ever become teachers. And we said "We shall see.", because we are fools.

To be fair, we aren't only fools; we'd had experiences the sceptics lacked, in successful endeavours in communities in disarray in Canada, and we'd had, in ways that make for other stories, more interaction with the type of women we meant to target, and we'd recognized the intelligence we'd expected to find unused or misused within them, seen the promise lying fallow in their darling children. If these aid workers had ever joked with a street beggar, rather than just brushed past her, or opened their foreclosing expectations, they might have seen what we'd seen.

We'd originally established Amarok Society as a registered charity working toward improvements in educational opportunities for aboriginal children in Canada. When Tanyss was brought to Ottawa as Senior Advisor to the Minister of Indian Affairs, Amarok Society became a conflict of interest, and we stowed it away in mothballs.

We wrote to AS' previous, extraordinary chairwoman, Angela, and asked if she was game to revive it as an organization providing education programmes to the poorest people of the poorest region on earth, and she, amazingly, immediately replied that she was. O, that's a moment she must revisit.

The latter-day legend of AS tells how Tanyss Madam and Gem Sir were sitting on the veranda at the Canadian Club, wondering how on earth to proceed with their inspired, innovative, impracticable idea, when at that very time Jalal bhai, the jovial manager of the club, approached them with uncharacteristic hesitancy and seriousness, and asked if he might speak to them on a most important matter. Knowing that their dues were fully paid up, Tanyss Madam invited him to proceed. He told them of a remarkable financial institution of his neighbourhood, a cooperative of poor women that had, through eighteen years, very quietly become the largest women's organization in the land, and, with 40,000 depositors and members, the largest women's financial institution in Asia, yet unseen and unknown. (When an article about it was submitted to Wikipedia, it was expunged as preposterous fiction.) Its manager, a Christian gentleman named Nittya, had polled the membership with the question "What can we do to improve your lives further?", and the answer had come with a resounding uniformity: "To improve our lives, we must learn English." (English has become so necessary to any hope of success here, as in India, the British High Commissioner to BD, himself a native-born Bangladeshi, cited English as a fundamental human right that isn't being met.) Nittya bhai had no connection whatsoever to anything English or international, and the only person he knew who had was Jalal bhai; and Jalal bhai's feet, or Destiny, had marched him straight over to the Munros, the only people of whom he'd even thought, and about whom he'd heard some talk of charitable educational endeavour: he hated to ask, but would they, could they, possibly consider undertaking a programme to teach very poor women? The legend tells how Gem Sir said "Funny you should ask."

Within the next few days, Jalal took us to meet Nittya and to show us the cooperative's operation. The office had an unimpressive entrance gate between two of a row of small open-front shops, but, behind a narrow passage, it opened into a large room divided into sections by windowed walls. At the time we were there, hundreds of poor women were lined up, most holding their week's deposit of about two dollars, before five or six wickets, behind which other poor women, obviously efficient, calmly received or handed out bills and registered transactions on bundled sheets or in large ledgers. It might have been from the nineteenth century. There wasn't an electronic device in the place. Behind a separate wicket was the accountant, a young woman named Ruma, who was to enter our first class and, later, play an essential role in AS' accomplishments.

When we spoke to international people about our planned programme, some warned us that the financial institution was surely some fly-by-night scam, and that we should keep our distance, to which we asked, do you

104

think a fly-by-night scam invites Canadians to educate its membership? Um, maybe not.... I mention that as indicative of how progress doesn't get made here.

It wasn't surprising that the first members or associates of the cooperative, or 'samity', to enrol in our English course should prove to be, overall, the most ambitious, daring and progressive of those qualified. Although the majority were women, we admitted some men and boys who were of members' families. One of the qualifications was a willingness to learn not only English, but also to teach English to members enrolling in future courses; by that means of multiplication, we meant to make English available to any member who wanted to learn it.

Tanyss, our children and I came to the first class full of Canadian industry and absence of ornamentation, all set to launch into the first lesson right away, foolishly overlooking the local love of ceremony and sense of occasion. This was a most important initiative, and they, quite rightly, weren't about to let it go unmarked. Nittya spoke first to the crowded classroom, extensively, in Bangla, of course, with many references to Dr. Tanyss and Mr. Gem. Then the President of the board of the Samity spoke at length, and when she was done, the deeply-respected Founding President was called upon, and she knew what she was doing; she seemed to deliver a long, detailed history of the Samity, reminding all present of her crucial part; it was a speech worth walking to hear, and it was warmly received. Then Jalal was introduced to give an account of his part in bringing us all together.

Then Nittya called upon Tanyss and me to favour them with a speech. With a hand to the small of my back, Tanyss surreptitiously pushed me forward; I knew what she was up to; it would fall to me to deliver a spontaneous speech, after which, she would say "Gem has said all I might have said." I could see her already running the phrase through her mind, a faint, pleased smile playing at the corners of her lips.

With Jalal translating, I spoke in congratulation of those who'd enrolled, of the critical role education must play in the development of beloved Bangladesh, and how, by their enrolment, they were assuming responsibility for the homeland's recovery. It was a real crowd-pleaser, as welcome as a rat swimming down the open street-side sewers. My innate Canadian modesty had failed us all: there they were, convened for their first chance ever to hear from a foreigner, and what did I talk about? Them. They already knew about themselves. They were there to hear about us, with braggadocio not only condoned but encouraged. Their applause was of that polite kind that very much emphasizes that it is polite. Realizing my deficiency, I turned to Tanyss, and told her it fell to her to try to win their interest with a fulsome relation of our experience and qualifications. Possibly, a faint, pleased smile played at the corners of my lips.

For the most part, those enrolled were of an age, all in their early to mid-twenties. The group was bracket by two notable exceptions: 15 year-old Farzana, and forty-ish Rohima. Farzana was the daughter of the samity President, and Rohima was, by then, a comfortably-ensconced housewife of the lower middle-class. She was far from well-off by our standards, but, through her careful economy, her family had a sufficient and varied diet of her very good cooking, an adequate flat, an adequate wardrobe, and her two young daughters were engaged in the pursuit of the odious 'O' Levels and appalling 'A' Levels at their adequate school. She was somewhat stout, and wore bare-midriff sarees to reveal her girth and, therefore, her family's relative prosperity, as befits a proper wife.

Neither Farzana nor Rohima had any English at all when they began our classes, and I sometimes, early on, wondered if they would become discouraged and quit, but they both saw it through, and learned rapidly, Farzana through natural ability, and Rohima through diligence.

Farzana is a stunning, flawless beauty; Rohima's beauty, of warmth, humour, generosity and compassion, shines from within, but is no less readily observed. She became our class' Auntie, and everyone loved her.

During one lesson, I asked each student his motivation for joining the class. Rohima's answer, that she wished to learn English to help her husband in his business, displeased Iqbal, an enlightened, forward-looking young man. "No, no," he said on behalf of Rohima's liberation, "you must not see yourself only as your husband's helper." This notion left Rohima confused. I suggested that, by learning English to help her husband's business, she was making a real economic contribution to her family, and that her reason was quite legitimate. Iqbal, who's very bright and reasonable, conceded with an easy tilt of his head.

During a later lesson, we were discussing a newspaper article about a panel of experts addressing Dhaka's many ills and dysfunctions. I asked each student, in turn, to say what her first task would be, were she mayor of Dhaka. The answers were, as always, thoughtful and aware, housing, health, education, political reform, but Rohima, the sensible housewife, took the prize when she stated simply "Firstly, I would give Dhaka a good cleaning." Of course, we all realized, no other enterprise could succeed until dirty Dhaka had a good cleaning. The experts on the panel had missed it, too.

When Tanyss and I were ready to open our first AS school for slum mothers, we told our Samity class members about the project; I knew that none of them had ever ventured into such a desperate and dangerous squatters' settlement as the site of this school. It was remarkable how readily and naturally those students, and then Nittya and the Samity board members, assumed their partnership in our strange effort.

We asked if there were anyone there whom we might hire as an assistant at the school, and at once, to our delighted surprise, Maksuda put herself forward as a candidate. She's a lovely young woman, quiet and self-possessed but humorous, very bright and conscientious. She told us that she was a "domesticated girl" and would, therefore, need to get permission from her parents. We told her to tell them that she'd never be required to enter the slum by herself, and on that assurance, and her parents' trust in us, she obtained the permission, and she was hired.

She blew her first pay packet on sweets for the Samity class.

Maksuda's reports to the class of the hardships and heartbreaks of our slum mothers, of the mothers' amazing dedication and progress in their school, and of how dearly she was coming to love them and their children, helped arouse in these very poor, struggling young people a deep concern and compassion for those they called 'the poor'. By degrees, the Samity class became the de facto AS slum teacher training programme, and brilliant Ruma took on such responsibility, it was inevitable we formalize her position as our executive officer.

As our first slum school stumbled to demonstrable success, our Samity students began to look about themselves with a different perspective, and some came to us with proposals for sites for new schools, usually in slums near their own houses. (Dhaka has three hundred slums.) As our meagre resources permitted, we opened new schools, with now-trained students of the Samity programme as our teachers.

Farzana, who could have parlayed her exceptional beauty into a better life of middle-class ease, instead aimed her life the other way, and became a teacher in a slum school.

And as for Rohima, quiet, calm, sensible Rohima reached into her deep-running, still, warm waters and pulled out a practical plan to a daring humanitarian end.

She arranged for us to visit a slum near her flat, and to meet with mothers with whom she had spoken about a school. In her careful, unhurried way, she told us how she longed to help the people there.

The meeting was held in one woman's home, a little tin and bamboo shanty lit by lantern and crammed with about forty women sitting on the palm-matted floor. As usual in these situations, Tanyss, Ruma and I were given the place of honour, on the one bed. Rohima waited by the door. I recall that the night was especially hot, but the women waited patiently. One woman stood by Tanyss throughout the visit, continually fanning her. Nittya arrived, and made a nice speech about Amarok Society, about us, and about the Samity. Ruma also spoke, and then I spoke, thanking Rohima for bringing the neighbourhood to our attention, and telling the women about what we did with our schools. I told them that the mothers in our schools understood that they were learning in order to teach, and the women all nodded seriously. Then I asked if such a thing was of interest to them.

One very thin, very handsome woman said that she was a labourer at construction sites, that she worked

109

every day, and still she couldn't afford to send her three children to school. "Learning to be their teacher is the answer to my problem," she said.

I asked her, "Do you mean that you are willing to work all day as a labourer, then come to our school in the evening, and then teach your children?"

"Yes, yes," she said, and several women in the room nodded with her.

At the end of the meeting, as we stood, the women stood, too, as a show of respect. One older woman rushed forward and hugged me, then backed away, head down, embarrassed, smiling still.

"Rohima apa," we said, once we'd found our sandals in the dark passageway between the hovels and were making our way to Wahid and our rickshaw waiting on the main road, "one way or another, you've got your school. Who do you see as being a good teacher for it?"

"But I wish to be the teacher," she said.

"Really?"

She nodded and smiled as though it were a marvellous surprise to her, too.

We hired her for the new school, and assigned another teacher, as well, a young firecracker named Rony who is so energetic, humorous, charming, and of such sparkling good looks, all the women in his other school are utterly enamoured of him when they don't want to kill him.

Amarok Society legend tells how, when women at its first slum school were being threatened and beaten by husbands for their attendance, Gem Sir went with his two big sons, Azien bhai and Gabriel bhai, and made it known to the husbands that, if there were any more threats or beatings, the offending husband would be taken away by the police, never to return home. Ruma apa was there to translate the message, and she reported it widely.

110

Rohima was always a good, thorough student, even of the AS legend.

And here is where the lines of these histories intersect:

Our schools aren't just innovative in their objectives, they're innovative in their teaching method, too: we teach literacy through songs, and not only is our method exceptionally effective, it's wholly consanguine to people always bursting with the song inside them. Whenever I visit a school, the women insist that I lead them in singing the alphabet, a nostalgic harkening back to our earliest days together, and I might be Pavarotti for the pleasure it brings them; A-B-C is my greatest hit. Our schools are very happy places.

With her happy school in place and operating, Rohima took Rony and, fourteen years after first pleading on poor Rabeya's behalf, she returned to Fatima's house, and, in her calm and careful way, she stood at the doorway and said this:

"I am an employee of a Canadian NGO and teacher at their school. If you don't release your daughter Rabeya to attend our school every day, I'll call the mental health authorities and they'll prove that Rabeya is normal and you're the abnormal one, and then I'll have you turned over to the police."

I wish I'd been there to see the look on two faces, Fatima's as she gaped upon Rohima returning in success to complete what she'd begun fourteen years earlier, and Rabeya's as she was led from her cell, clothed and placed in Rohima's care by her terrified mother.

It took incredible devotion and patience on Rohima's and Rony's part, but a year and a half after Rabeya was first brought, timid, shrinking, crying, into the school, a visitor would never guess that the woman confidently reading both Bangla and English in front of her classmates, interacting normally with them throughout the lesson, laughing with the others at Rony's clever jokes, had undergone such an horrific ordeal. Perhaps an astute visitor might perceive some special tenderness in the way Rabeya regards her teacher Rohima.

We are in the business of going where we can't go and doing what can't be done, of teaching mothers to teach their children and their neighbours' children. However, we're flexible, and we make exceptions. Sometimes we'll enrol a girl, a daughter of a mother who would attend, but is prevented by sweatshop overtime, and so on, so that the girl can teach her sisters and brothers.

Sometimes we'll admit a woman who isn't a mother for reasons that fall outside the very wide range of normal to which we've had to adapt.

Amarok Society legend tells how Rohima auntie enrolled in an English class because she wanted to help her family, and how she found a far bigger family and far greater opportunity to help than she'd ever imagined. The legend tells how she eschewed easy comfort and transformed herself into a woman heroic, so to help other heroic women who'll labour all day and then overcome bone-weariness to learn and teach all evening, how she made herself heroic, so to defy arrayed ironclad tyrannies, to rescue from its dark cell an heroic blossom of life's surpassing determination to renew itself wherever it may, and a demonstration that where there is life, there is hope.

The Eid of Destruction

My sweetheart and I spent some years running a cattle ranch (running often being the operative word) in the wilderness of the Canadian Rockies. Our thundering herd roamed through the savage forest, facing its vicissitudes, and was pretty much feral, very unlike the herds to be seen within central Canadian fenced fields; ours were malcontents to a cow, and were active, hot-tempered and, we thought, a lot smarter than the more domesticated variety: how else to explain how often they outsmarted us? To our observation, they each had bovine personality to burn. We liked them very much, even while cursing them to the peaks of the surrounding mountains. We called them The Bucolic Plague.

One autumn day, the owner of a big steer of the herd came out to the ranch to slaughter it, and he brought along some of his pals for the fun. To make a long and painful story short and painful, this killing crew decided that the most entertaining method of slaughter was to shoot the steer with their rifles, hunt it through the forest as they would a deer. Alas for the steer, they weren't the great white hunters they fancied, and they potted at it, whooping and racing after it, wounding it several times before finally bringing it down just outside our cabin. They were shooting in the direction of our cabin, without warning, to do it.

Before hauling the carcass away in their pick-up, the steering committee cut off the head and tossed it aside.

When Tanyss and I ventured out from under the bed and went outside, we found some of the surviving members of the herd standing in a defensive circle around the head, in the way that musk-oxen defend their lambs against threats, with their rumps in and their horns out, their heads lowered. Even though the herd and we usually enjoyed a cordial relationship, good-hearted friendship, even, we were thereby condemned as a species, and bulls and cows alike feinted at us with menace.

Tanyss and I decided it would be prudent to withdraw into our cabin until heads cooled, if you'll excuse the term in the circumstance. From inside, we heard the herd moo-mourning and low-lamenting throughout the night.

The experience was another big step toward our conversion into that rarity, the cowboy who won't eat red meat.

The yahoos with rifles were, I recall, slices of white-loaf Pentecostal. I mention that so it will be understood that any tone of censure that might inadvertently creep into the following story should be seen as being, as with our cattle, directed at an entire species rather than a race, religion or culture.

If a traveller, or a cow, heads west, north or east in Bangladesh, he (or in the case of a cow, she) will eventually come to India. As with Canada and the U.S., the border between the two is not always clearly marked; however, a handy rule of thumb is that if the land is as flat as Saskatchewan and under constant threat of floods and/or erosion and/or typhoons and/or tidal waves, it's Bangladesh, and if it's reasonably stable and has any topography deserving of the term, it's India. And if I'm ever negotiating a partition, myself, I want the Indian team on my side.

Muslim Bangladeshis don't eat pork, and Hindu Indians don't eat beef. But whereas cattle are at liberty to wander through Delhi, the countless impromptu garbage piles of Dhaka are available to the crows, rats and goats undisturbed by any pigs at all, for nary a single trotter

114

sets itself upon this land; anyone debating whether he'd do better being thought of as sacred or as unclean might note that.

We have stood at the border of Bangladesh in the northeast and watched cattle doomed to curry masala grazing in a field on our side, apparently content, where the tiniest triumph of curiosity or wanderlust over immediate appetite would have carried them across a shallow river to sanctuary and bovine nirvana.

I used those cattle to illustrate to my children what complacency would do for them.

In Muslim Bangladesh there are two annual Eids, religious celebrations, that are observed in a major way. One, Eid ul-Fitr, celebrates the conclusion of Ramadan, the period of fasting every autumn. Now, the great majority of Bangladeshis never get enough to eat, to the point where, it is estimated, two-thirds of the population have suffered stunting, where their long bones are insufficiently nourished to follow the genetic blueprint, so a period of fasting every year for them might seem as necessary as a dehumidifier in the Sahara, but they observe it scrupulously for the most part. Mohammed (PBUH) was a practical prophet, and there are exemptions, but the rule is that no food or drink is to be taken between sun-up and sundown. Strict Muslims won't even swallow their saliva, and spend daylight hours spitting on the streets and footpaths, producing the least natural of the seasonal floods. Given that respiratory complaints are pandemic in Dhaka, due to the air pollution, the footpaths are already heel deep in spit and phlegm; during Ramadan, the level rises to ankle-deep.

The very small percentage of Bangladeshis who are wealthy, absurdly wealthy, have worked out the Ramadan fast to their advantage. Anyone who can acquire multi-multiples of their fair share in a land where there isn't

115

nearly enough to go around won't let the requirements of his religion interrupt his appetites and comforts; what the wealthy do is prepare (or have their servants prepare) a big meal at 4:00 am, which they tuck into until sunrise. This tides them over until a signal, usually a bell, tells them that the sun has officially set, at which time they eat an array of traditional deep-fried treats to break their fast, and then they follow that up with a hearty meal. For the wealthy, Ramadan is the fast during which they eat more than usual, and then they celebrate Eid al-Fatr.

Tanyss and I had a curious experience when we went to our favourite restaurant one evening during Ramadan. Our timing was a bit erroneous, and we were ushered into a dining room of about another hundred people who were already seated in quiet anticipation of the signal that hadn't yet come. We were seated, and Sayed, the maitre d', signalled and the traditional break-fast treats were brought to our table with what I felt was an unwarranted flourish, and five waiters gathered around us, probably not for the purpose of drawing attention to us. We were quite capable of waiting until the signal was sounded: Tanyss and I generally only eat one meal a day, after sundown, and, anyway, we'd been swallowing saliva all day, so we were fine. The waiters, however, would have none of our intended courtesy. "Eat, eat," they exhorted us. "You're not Muslim. Eat, eat!" They seemed so concerned for us, as though they feared we might slip from our chairs in a starvation faint, we were compelled to begin. We ate under the watchful gaze of all the lip-licking others. I don't believe I've ever eaten so noisily so unwillingly. Every swallow seemed to resound through the room like a kettle-drum, and the self-conscious trauma has created a false --- surely --- memory of my ogre-ish belch bouncing off the walls. I detected no resentment in the attentive onlookers, though; I got the impression we were their surrogate eaters, but maybe we just nicely emphasized their pious virtue.

Eid ul-Fitr is a benign feast, if rather excessive in commercial terms as the wealthy find in it an excuse to treat themselves to the conspicuous consumption of expensive electronics and clothing. The second main Eid, Eid al Adha, on the other hand, commemorates Ibrahim's willingness to obey Allah's order to sacrifice Ismael, commemorates it in a way I'd really rather it didn't.

According to Muslim belief, Ibrahim (Abraham to Jews and Christians) had two sons, Ismael and Isaac; followers of Islam are descended from Ismael, and Hebrews are descended from Isaac. Muslims have Allah calling upon Ibrahim to sacrifice Ismael, while Hebrews have Jehovah calling on Abraham to sacrifice Isaac. According to some accounts, the boy was reprieved at the last moment, and Ibrahim/Abraham slaughtered a ram instead, and it is this that Muslims emulate at Eid al Adha.

In Dhaka, this manifests itself with the importation of even more cattle and goats into the city, where those who have the means buy them at inflated prices for the purpose of sacrificing them in the streets. It is the custom that the animals are bought several days in advance and are then tethered in display outside the fences of the purchasers' homes; not all purchasers are fastidious in cleaning up behind the cattle and goats, and navigating the streets takes on yet heightened adventure.

Across the street from our second flat in Dhaka (which we eventually ceded to the invading hordes of cockroaches), there was a privately-owned palatial white mansion, a leftover from the colonial Raj era, with large black cast-iron lions still recumbent in confident power beside the gleaming white columns, where large goldfish still curled through an illuminated green pond, where bent groundsmen clipped the lawn with small scissors, where an Art Nouveau tulip-shaped, brass and glass elevator rose and descended silently through the mansion's five storeys; we knew all this because our balcony was high enough for us to look over the high white wall surrounding the place and through the large windows and the French windows opening onto the numerous patios and balconies.

There were three oddities occupying the grounds within the walls. Two were dogs, young German shepherds, or Alsatians as they would have been called there; these dogs were so different from the scabrous, mangy, quivering, skinny dogs that roamed the streets, they might have been from a different world, and so they were. Such dogs were, rarely, imported as status symbols. The third oddity was the young man charged with the dogs' training and care; in a land of tiny people whom deprivation was still shrinking, this fellow was a giant of over six feet, and muscular, and unusually dark. Ostensibly, he was the dog-handler and a security guard, but in reality, he was a status symbol as much as the dogs.

I very seldom saw the mansion's latest owner, a short, stout Bangladeshi man. We'd been told he was making a mountain of money as a real estate developer; he made enough to absent himself and his family from Dhaka most of the time, and usually his staff of servants had the run of the place, the aforementioned peons with their gardening scissors, the maids who came out to the fifth floor patio to hang their own laundry, the chauffeurs who brought the various Mercedes and SUVs out from the underground garage to wash them when they didn't need it, to drive them pointlessly 'round and 'round the block, the other security guards, uniformed and armed at the back gate who saluted me whenever I walked by.

118

The young giant didn't wear a uniform. He was dressed always in a cotton lungi which he'd usually gathered up between his legs to form a sort of loin cloth; sometimes he wore an old beige t-shirt or, on chilly nights, a sweater, but normally he went shirtless. He never went inside the mansion. He slept on its columned front porch, between Alsatians and lions, without any mat. He very seldom ventured outside the gate, usually only to buy a cigarette and maybe a biscuit or piece of sweet toast from a wandering vendor. (Most Bangladeshi men smoke, but poverty limits most of them to two or three cigarettes a day, bought one at a time from the circling vendors.) He smoked his cigarettes the way other Bangladeshi men do, with great care and concentration.

I would see him in the mornings, as the sun rose, when the street was still and the city quiet but for the birds awakening in the trees, as I stood on my balcony drinking my tea, he would rouse himself, stretching, and would undertake some simple exercises that consisted of him swinging bricks around. The street between us was typically narrow, and I could detect him watching me from the corner of his eye.

One morning, as he was taking a sidelong inspection, I gave him a wave of acknowledgement. He was visibly startled. Both his country's constitution and his religion are officially egalitarian, but in practical terms that means nothing; the caste structure here is as durable and iron-clad as the lions on the porch. So my disruption of it that morning unsettled him, and only after a moment did he begin to raise his hand in return, hesitantly, as though I might yet snub his presumption. I waved again, and he smiled widely. It became customary for us to greet each other with waves in the early mornings, when it seemed the rest of the city still slept.

One morning, he actually spoke.

"Tea?" he asked.

"Yes, tea," I said, raising my cup.

He nodded several times with happy satisfaction at the discussion, which he apparently regarded as thorough and complete. I suspect he'd exhausted his English vocabulary.

About a week before Eid al Adha, workmen constructed a sort of canopy of bright material and a hitching post along the western wall of the mansion ---- it's on a corner and fronts two streets, one to its west and one to its south. It was northward across the south-facing wall I would look ---- and a day later there were trotted to it eight enormous Brahman steers, long-legged, pale grey, shoulder-humped, with deep dark pool eyes in which one might almost spot the glimmer of goldfish, and along with them were led five black goats. The friendly giant was charged with their care.

Eventually, the goats were taken within the wall and tied to the rungs of a ladder laid out on the lawn. This seemed to be for the convenience of the sons of the owner, two boys of ten and twelve who were, like their father, dull-eyed, short and rotund, and who enjoyed tormenting the goats with sticks or any other instrument that fell to their chubby hands. The goats danced around and cried like children, and I wondered why Allah had lately wholly suspended the occasionally useful practice of ordering fathers to kill sons. The giant would watch the poking boys poker-faced, but when they were bored by their cruelty and listlessly gone, he would patiently unravel and untangle the goats' tethers.

The steers were decorated with rosettes at their ears and foreheads, and with marigold garlands around their necks. They were sometimes harassed by the mangy street curs, but mainly their last days were spent sedately chewing and defecating, mindless of the hideous horror to come.

Below our west-facing balcony, four much smaller cattle arrived a few days later without fanfare. Garlands were placed around their necks, but they weren't bedecked with the rosettes of their more impressive brethren along the street. These were the more modest sacrifices of the well-to-do residents of our apartment building, and they served, by comparison, to demonstrate the inherent lie in the overstatement of our wealthy neighbour; for to the passer-by, he was boasting "See how rich I am, that I can dispense with so much.", while to Allah he was saying "See how pious and obedient I am, that I will suffer to sacrifice so much." It would be a convenient Allah indeed whose omniscience could falter long enough to miss the intrinsic contradiction.

On the morning of the grisly day itself, the dark giant appeared decked out in a clean long shirt and a new prayer cap, moving carefully within his unusual raiment.

Our upstairs neighbour, a businessman, turned out in his fine embroidered attire to inspect his small brown cow. He happened to look up to our balcony, and saw Tanyss and me watching him.

"Please, sister and brother, stay inside your flat today," he called up to us. "This is too disturbing for you. Please."

We thanked him for his concern and withdrew; we didn't doubt that we would be disturbed (many of the few westerners here arrange trips away from Dhaka to avoid Eid al Adha), but we also knew the unquiet urgencies of our hungry eyes, and we went out to our north-facing balcony instead.

The mansion's owner and his family were arrayed on balconies of two levels, their corpulence in shimmering golden embroidery. Father and boys stood together, and round women and girls were grouped together separately.

On the street were perhaps two dozen skinny hired men, naked but for the cotton wound around their crotches. One of them was whetting a long knife, and others were ravelling and unravelling jute ropes, while the remainder stood waiting. The owner began reciting prayers, referring to a small sheet in his hand. The others of his family, male and female alike, seemed to be exploring how high their noses and how low their eyelids could go at the same time in sneering display of their superb haughtiness. They looked ridiculous beyond my powers to resist.

"Look at them," I said to Tanyss. "They don't eat pork because they've a squeamish aversion to cannibalism."

"Don't insult pigs," Tanyss said. We used to raise pigs, and we liked them, too.

An imam arrived, sharpening his own long knife, and the first steer was led around the corner from the hitching rail on the west-facing wall to the south-facing wall, right under our balcony. Some of the little men took a rope and tied it around the steer's foreleg, and then pulled it around the other legs, then began to pull it closed. At a command from one of them, they pulled hard on the tightening rope while other men launched themselves at the steer's side, and then down it went. It tried to rise again, but the men gathered together its hooves within the cinching rope, and another man dove onto its head.

Its tongue shot in and out of its mouth, and its eyes strained.

The men took a long time tying a number of ropes, and the steer cooperatively demonstrated where more restriction was required.

122

Several men leant in to press their lightweight downward on the steer's frame. The imam stepped forward and indicated with his knife where on the steer's neck he would cut, and two men extended the loose hide on either side of the spot.

The imam said a prayer, then cut a nick, and then sawed through the throat to the spinal column, where he stopped.

The steer sent little men bouncing.

The amount of blood in one of those animals is astounding, as is the ongoing imperative of its system to somehow sustain its life. The heart beat and beat, as evidenced by the crimson jets into the street, the chest heaved and heaved, sending out blatting exhalations, trying to suck in air, and on and on it kicked within its bonds. I don't know how long it was alive, but it didn't seem dead for ten minutes at least. The sons of the mansion laughed at it throughout.

Other men started the heavy job of skinning the first steer as the second was being led past it, through the gore. This represented a flaw in their plan, as the steers were in turn led past and through a longer and longer corridor of carnage, and became, in turn, more and more agitated.

The sixth steer was largest of them all, and became most rampant as it was led by the remains of the five earlier sacrifices. When the men tried to wrap a rope around its legs, it had enough, and it bucked, throwing men away, and stepped out of the snare. It was free and unencumbered.

The ladies of the mansion screamed and threw up their hands, as though its first motivation would be to somehow mount the wall, scale their balcony, and do them harm. The father and sons shouted recriminations at the men, who darted in with ropes to be repelled by threatening horns; these men, who were probably to be paid about two dollars each for their days' heavy labour, obviously reckoned there were better ways of wasting one's life, and withdrew to a safe distance.

The big steer stepped about in some indecision.

The father gesticulated urgently and demanded something of the dark young giant, who nodded calmly and removed his prayer cap and squirmed out of his long shirt, handing them to a man standing beside him, and stepped into the middle of the street to confront the rogue steer. The sight of the young man seemed to settle the steer's swirling confusion, gave it an immediate objective in life, that being to elude the young man.

If anyone watching had bothered to notice the steers' extreme reluctance to step in the blood of their fellows, the escape route of the rogue might have been easily anticipated, and what little of the street wasn't awash in blood might have been blocked. As it was, the young giant positioned himself precisely where the steer wouldn't wish to go, at the far end of a wide pool. The steer charged down the single dry path, and got by the lunging young man without difficulty and broke for freedom.

"Run!" I called to it from our balcony. "Run, run, you poor fool!" (See * below), and Tanyss took up the call.

Other people wailed in dismay.

The fat little sons berated the young giant.

What happened next was one of the most remarkable things I've ever seen:

The sons of the house, with the reckless hubris of those whose view of the world is severely limited by the raising of the nose and the constant near-closing of the eyes, a pitiable affliction affecting mainly the very rich, cast little golden lassoes around the passing steer's neck. They have miscalculated, however, underestimated the determination of the steer or overestimated its natural obedience to innate privilege, and even their exceptional combined weight isn't sufficient to contain the brute, and they are jerked forward, pulled from their balcony as their father gapes behind them, and, tragically, their spongy midriffs are impaled on the wrought-iron spikes Father had set into the top of the white wall to keep the rabble out; their blue blood mingles with the red of the street; the servants are maddened with grief at what has befallen their young masters (or, rather, what they have befallen), so hysterical that their wails sound strangely like rousing cheers. Even the goats join this lament, bleating with a despair so distracted that it would, in happier circumstances, be construed as capricorny laughter.

The steer reaches the corner of the street, and is about to turn northward, when it catches sight of our upstairs neighbour's pretty little sacrificial cow, about which men are just now gathering with ropes. I alone have observed, over the past days, the budding bovine rapport between these two as they stood tethered on the street, the first shy glances on her part, his increasingly overt nods and waggles of his great white head, the batting of her long lashes, the manly pawing of his mighty hoof, the saucy sway of her rump roast, or whatever.

He lowers his horns and charges at those who threaten her, and the men scatter like flies from a whishing tail. Our neighbour cries that now matters have become too disturbing for him, too, and he scrabbles up a handy mahogany tree, and I notice that he's unusually adroit for an import/export consultant.

125

Together, the steer and cow rush up the street, bellowing to the remaining two steers to follow, who yank so sharply on their ropes that they snap the hitching rail, and the four carry on up the street, mooing in rebellious triumph.

They rampage through the city, liberating sacrificial cattle as they find them. Ashen imams disavow any knowledge of the long knives in the dust at their feet. The numbers of the saved swell to thousands of roaming, vengeful kine, and the human inhabitants cower within doors. As an obvious non-Muslim, I dare to go out to assess the situation. The air booms with mooing celebration.

I pick my way through the pie-sized booby-traps laid down by the renegades, and, turning a corner, I suddenly find myself face-to-face with the big steer, if he can be said to have a face. Beside him is the little brown cow, and behind them are thousands of hostile, glaring cattle.

On either side of me are walls too high to scale.

"I don't even like Hemingway," I say bitterly. Even in such a dire strait, my turn of obscure literary reference doesn't fail me. Of course, I doubt that the steer actually understands English*, let alone precious attempts to frame life as merely a metaphor for literature.

So I stand in the hemming way (there I go again!), and the steer lowers its horns and snorts and hooves the dirt, and I wonder if I might turn over a new Munro Leaf (there I go again, I'm irrepressible!), when, in desperation, I say:

"I'm the one who shouted to you to run...." (See * above). As a precaution, I omit reference to the "poor fool" part of my exhortation.

Perhaps something in the sound of my voice triggers a memory. He raises his head and stares at me

126

intently. Then, slowly, silently, he moves to one side of the street, and the cow moves with him. Then, in succession, with nothing to be heard but the clop-clop of their hooves and, overhead, the mournful caw of a crow for which this day has been a major disappointment, the cattle behind them move to either side of the street, creating a safe passage for me.

It isn't actually the way I want to go, but if they're going to be so deferential, I don't want to seem ungrateful, so I pass between them within their silent gaze. Scarcely am I through than the kine clarion call to freedom moos again, and the stampede is on once more.

According to the newspapers, the herd departs Dhaka and migrates to the northeast, collecting cattle as it goes; it is last seen crossing a river into the promised land of India, wakening to liberation the last cattle that had been, up to this time, complacently grazing in the field just on the Bangladesh side. Seen at the head of the massive exodus is a tall pale steer, and cleaved to his side is a small brown cow.

Of course, it might be necessary for the cow to compromise her dearest girlish hopes in the days ahead, as she is, after all, cleaved to a steer, not a bull, but that still beats being cleaved by an imam's blade.

All right, so, in truth that was one of the most remarkable things I've never seen.

What really happened was that the steer rounded the corner and, with open road in front of it, it lined itself up at the hitching rail with the two remaining steers, and there it stood in perfect compliance, eating hay, until the young giant came and tied another rope around its neck and secured it to the rail. They let it skip a turn before they took it and slaughtered it.

To sacrifice the goats, the men would just sit on them while the throats were cut. There was no sense of ceremony with the goats. They were done in almost as an afterthought, but they cried like children, and the way their thin, knobbly legs raced frantically as they died, something inside them seemed to hold an imperative that their little lives counted for something, too.

The skinny men worked through the hot day skinning the carcasses and cutting them into sections, and carrying the sections to the back gate, from where they were taken indoors. The men were all covered in blood, like the streets of Dhaka.

At our dinner that evening, which consisted most definitely of foods that had never had a throat to be cut, I told my children the regrettable true story of the steer that broke away.

"If any of you think you'll find some measure of security by trying to blend into the crowd, let this be a lesson to you," I concluded. "Your only hope is through the deliberate and unflagging pursuit of freedom, for yourself and everyone."

Of course, I was preaching to the choir. My children are such rugged individualists, they regard Thoreau as unfortunately conformist.

As we were finishing our dinner, we heard a sudden swell of angry voices outside, from the side of the mansion.

Tanyss and I went out to the balcony to see.

At the back gate of the mansion, a large crowd was gathered.

It's prescribed that the meat from the sacrificial animal is to be divided into three equal portions: one third is to be kept, one third is to be given to neighbours, and one third is to be given to the poor.

We were the neighbours; we correctly assumed that there would be no meat coming the way of our apartment building, so the owner had contrived a double share already; but there was still the disposition of a third ration to the poor, and the poor had made note of the owner's self-aggrandizing display through the week, and during the course of the Eid day, over a hundred representatives, people who normally have nothing to eat but rice and lentils day after day, collected to await the singular annual treat to the appetite that never abates, and what the Qur'an insisted was to be theirs.

It was a long time coming. It was well after dark, and well after the owners had set into their own feast in the great glittering dining room behind the crystal French windows, that the distribution had begun.

The uproar, which increased as we watched, was from the crowd's growing realization that what were being passed out through the gate were tiny chunks of beef about two inches cubed, at a ration of one chunk per person.

The protest rose to a storm. Above the roar outside the gate, individual voices could be heard, almost singing, in denunciation, and from inside the gate, other voices in high alarm and warning. Hands shook the gate with fury, and other hands behind it nervously fingered rifles.

The air was electric and expectant, and shimmered white on shiny black.

Then at the gate there appeared the dark young giant, dressed once again in his finery for this one Eid day, but who all other days lived as a dog on the front porch, a naked domesticated brute; and like a black iron colonial lion, he stood in an attitude of near-repose, his arms folded, his head to one side, his eyes half-open, the better to emphasize his confidence in the terrible strength he held in reserve. On either side of him were the Alsatians.

The hands withdrew from the gate. Voices fell. A voice of conferred authority rose to reclaim control. The distribution of the meagre chunks began anew, and continued without further incident, and the people departed the mansion for their cramped hovels.

No faces ever filled the little bevelled panes of the French windows. No one ever rose from the splendid feast within to discover anything of the hungry turmoil without.

But I fancied that, at their table, the father was telling his children: "Let this be a lesson to you: the steer may threaten to break away, but in the end, it will return to its hitching rail and to its hay."

And in heaven, Allah's vision was so bedazzled by their golden embroidery, by the golden ware at their table....

For a long period of our lives, we fixed up the unhappiest schools in the unhappiest communities in Canada, communities of poverty, yes, but, more seriously, of degenerative hopelessness. One of the problems we confronted was of children from households in disarray arriving at school hungry. The solution to this problem, we felt, was obvious: we must feed the children at the school. However, at each school, we encountered vehement resistance from members of our teaching staff, fewer than half of them, perhaps, who argued that by feeding the children we were "letting the parents off the hook." Our position was that the parents weren't on the hook, weren't even nibbling at the bait, and that our not caring for the children would do nothing to cause the parents to put their lives in order, it would, if anything, only dig their pit deeper. By what logic does a parent's irresponsibility relieve us of our human responsibility?

130

By that token, though, I've been reluctant to talk about the very few, very wealthy moguls of Bangladesh, lest First World people decide that they shouldn't let the Third World wealthy off the hook by taking any humanitarian responsibility for the ongoing, sequential and chronic disaster. But then Gabriel says "Anyone who thinks that way wouldn't have helped us, anyway."

Consider this for First World responsibility:

Somewhere in the world not here, commodity manipulators caused the price of rice nearly to double in less than a year, merely by stating that it would. The mothers of our schools, the poorest people in the world, who live hand-to-mouth, suddenly found the hand half-empty, as with millions and millions of other hands left holding only half, not nearly enough for all those mouths. We watch as the thin become thinner, as the weak become weaker, as the sick become sicker, so that certain schemers can easily afford that sixth Mercedes, that fourth luxury estate. Why rice, of all commodities, the staple of humanity's poorest? They carelessly managed to cause more suffering than all the Bangladeshi moguls might have in their most wicked dreams.

Tanyss and I have sometimes been asked why or how we press on as we do in the most discouraging situations available to us, why or how we don't succumb to despair; perhaps we're being asked, politely, if we're insane.

The answer we give is that we are always finding encouragements to our hopes, bolsters to our beliefs.

We're given reasons to believe, for instance, that our young teachers are the future of Bangladesh and the world, not the porcine princelings to the palace born, that the obscenely wealthy fathers go on sacrificing their fatted sons unbidden, while we build the abilities of our tough, sinewy sons and daughters to go forth and give all they've received, not in one-third shares, but all, and then they, step-by-step, day-by-day, prove us right and thank us for the chance.

We're given reasons to believe in the courage of our students, our schools' mothers who defy tradition, fatigue, hunger and depression to take upon themselves the responsibility of learning to teach their own and others' children, and to believe in their children, who take to learning with an alacrity to evince that, despite all the information to the contrary, something inside them seems to hold an imperative that their little lives count for something, too.

We're given reasons to believe in the common decency prevalent around the world when our upstairs neighbour warns us compassionately to avert our eyes as he performs his sacred duty, and then still sends down to us our fair-share chunk of little brown cow, and on the next sabbath distributes not chunks of raw meat, but a fully prepared meal to all passing beggars.

We rely on our belief in the person half a world away from our programmes who can hear about them and never question what these efforts have to do with her, who can, without hesitation, understand human responsibility.

And we rely on our belief that for enough people, o, I don't know, maybe more than half of the people reading this, some part inside them, something in a chamber of their hearts, wished my absurd little story of the freedom-fighter steer to be true.

FARZANA

Grace Notes on Black and White Keys

There is, in the middle class enclave near where we live, a bakery with a café in an enclosed back section that we at first regarded as simply a bakery with a café. Tanyss and I didn't have any need to consider the strategic advantages of a nice café that had no exposure to the busy street before it.

The bakery was recommended to us as one that might be able to satisfy western tastes, to which it conscientiously seeks to appeal. Bangladeshis, in keeping with their general schizophrenia, are mad for two extremes in what they eat: spicy and sweet; street vendors do a brisk business in foot-long sections of sugar cane, the core of which people walk along munching; other vendors wheel around little presses that squeeze similar sections of sugar cane, and the syrup that flows out is sold as a drink. At tea stalls, if I ask for tea without sugar, the server regards it as his imperfect understanding of English and ignores what seems to be my absurd request, puts in extra sugar in case that's what I meant. Bread normally available is heaped with sugar; we've pretty much concluded that the only difference in brown and white bread is the colour of the sugar used. It's all enough to make one's teeth ache to withdraw beneath the gums.

Tanyss the optimist set Ratan to the task of baking bread. I the realist donated the resultant loaves to some children who work all day breaking bricks at a nearby construction site, to see if they could get any good out of them, maybe a miracle of the loaves and fissures.

And in more curiosity than high expectation, Tanyss and I made our way through the daytime heat to the recommended bakery, and, upon discovering the back-room café, we thought we'd restore ourselves there.

As we went in, we noticed immediately that all the small tables that were occupied were occupied by young couples, one young woman and one young man each; and each of the young men marked us sharply as we entered, but, more oddly, all the young women quickly lowered their heads, to conceal their faces behind shawls or the drapes of their hair.

We sat ourselves down at a free table, and as we waited to place our order, we observed the young women cautiously raising their eyes in assessment of whatever threat we might pose.

"This is a trysting place," Tanyss said.

"So it is," I said.

In BD, arranged marriages are the rule, and affianced couples often barely know each other, and are never alone together. Love matches are generally scorned as self-indulgent and disorderly, eliciting shame for two families so out of control; and, judging from letters to editors and youth columns, it's young people themselves who tend to be most strident in condemnation of the creeping westernized degeneration of love matches.

The couples around us were love matches, stealing moments together hidden from prying eyes and busybodies, speaking in short, intimate murmurs, daring to touch fingers beneath the tables, sighing, glorying in the heartache of unsanctioned romance.

I sighed, too.

"Remember how your parents detested me?" I asked Tanyss, touching her fingers beneath the table.

"Just despised you," she murmured dreamily. "And they still do."

"I know," I said. "Could it be any finer?"

She surreptitiously stroked my hand in the way that makes my heart leap.

The young gallants glanced at me from time to time in continuing suspicion.

"We could give them lessons in romance," I said. I didn't at that moment recognize it as a sort of imprecise prediction.

This is the part of the story where I slip into the sin of parental pride. It is utterly necessary to any understanding that I relate that our daughter, Grace, is rather the teenaged Canadian girl equivalent of the BD taste; by that I don't mean merely to suggest that she is both spicy and sweet, although she is both, but that she incorporates two extremes: she is extremely beautiful and extremely intelligent. My pride is based on my own achievement in producing such a marvel, that is, marrying a woman who is both extremes herself and then wisely contributing only recessive genes.

Shortly after we arrived in Dhaka, Tanyss and I undertook our duty to Grace's gifts by shopping around for an electronic piano and a school for her; the electronic piano was straightforward enough, as there seemed to be only one store in Dhaka that actually sold one. The selection of a suitable school proved to be almost as restrictive, in the end. The leading school, by all accounts, is the American International School, which is renowned as the best school in all South Asia, and the lesser, default option is the Grace School, which is Roman Catholic (so we deduced that the 'Grace' name wasn't a specific dedication to our daughter). As we're neither American nor Roman Catholic and had, apparently and as memory serves, resisted any passing fancies to become either one through the years, we weren't wholly pleased with our choices, but we chose the A.I.S.

Whether the A.I.S. chose us remained to be seen, as it has a rigorous selection process of its own. It is the cocoon of ambassadorial and neo-Mogul pupae, and isn't set up for just anyone.

As a tour demonstrated, once we had passed its stringent security to gain entry, the school was superbly equipped, right down to water fountains from which the students could actually drink without dire diseases ensuing. The very pleasant administrative assistant ushering Grace and me around said, "It's as though Dhaka isn't outside here at all. We live in a bubble here."

"O, well," I said in polite reassurance, "I'm sure that some local benefit penetrates the fortress-like walls."

She regarded me oddly.

In time, she turned us over to the guidance counsellor, who was also in charge of admissions. After an American attempt to break my hand, he sat us down. I told him that we wished to enrol Grace in grade nine.

"At her age, she should be entering grade eight," he said.

"By her academic achievements, she could be entering university," I said, "but we'll settle for grade nine."

"Grade nine is out of the question. Do you have the transcripts of her previous school?"

"I am her previous school," I said. "Since grade four, she's been privately educated."

I might have said that we raised her on a diet of raw rat, for the way he looked at me.

"What curriculum did you follow?" he demanded.

"Inadequacies of curricula were the very problem. She followed the British Columbia math curriculum, but her humanities studies were of my own design. My wish was that she pass from high school a learned person, and a public school education clearly wasn't going to accomplish that."

That the school is hermetically sealed against the stinks of Dhaka meant that the stinks of Munro so surprisingly released right there in his office couldn't be immediately vented, and he sputtered against them.

"What, what---- what have you been thinking of?!"

I glanced at Grace; she gave me her "he ended with a preposition" look.

"Well, I was trying to do what was best for my children's edu----."

But I was too vile to behold, and he made a show of cutting my monstrous, self-serving excuses short, and looked at my poor little girl, instead.

Americans, of course, are in the business of liberating, internationally, even liberating those who neither wish it nor need it, and as he looked at Grace, a very American resolve stole into his expression. He was going to liberate Grace from me, I could see.

"We might consider grade eight," he told her.

"Grade eight is a complete waste for a girl who's just finished 'Crime and Punishment'," I insisted.

He narrowed his eyes and turned to me once more, longing to punish my crime.

"You must have some process of assessment," I suggested.

In the tersest terms possible, he informed me that they used famously difficult entrance examinations from Australia, and that, if Grace sat them, her results would be compared not only to the results of A.I.S. students, but to all students around the world who used those exams. Clearly for the sole purpose of fully revealing my error, he agreed that Grace might attempt the grade nine level exams. He was obviously surprised when Grace said she was willing to take them on the spot.

He told me I could wait in the library, preferably not touching anything.

There was a sort of reluctant shuffle in his step when they came to get me a few hours later.

"How did it go?" I asked Grace.

She sighed.

"Well, she got ninety-nine percent," he said glumly.

"Only ninety-nine?" I asked Grace. She gave me her "he deducted a mark on principle" look.

"She was very well prepared," he begrudged.

"Actually, she wasn't prepared at all. She was educated."

He'd lost a bit of his liberational zeal, and deigned to downgrade my playing card from Saddam to maybe one of Saddam's slightly-less-guilty junior ministers, and in that manner described various aspects of parental responsibility to the school. Then he said "We live in a bubble here."

"Ah, well," I said in conciliatory encouragement, "I'm sure you're able to absorb some of the local flavour."

He regarded me oddly.

He spoke with genuine concern about exposing a hot-house flower like Grace to the rough and tumble of competitive and ambitious upper-crust diplobrats and plutobrats. I tried to assure him that his perception of her as a shrinking violet and social misfit was mistaken.

"But she tells me she doesn't even like hip-hop," he said worriedly. "Their music is very important to our students. She says she loves classical music."

"Is musical literacy enfeebling?" I asked. "Don't we believe that knowledge is empowering?"

"Maybe if she got to know some hip-hop," he suggested.

"Or brushed up on baby-talk," I suggested.

He took us to meet the principal, who apparently doubted the guidance counsellor's ability to pulverize

139

every bone in a Canadian hand, and set in to do a proper job.

Then he said "We live in a bubble here."

"Not to worry," I reassured him, "I'm sure elements of the exotic experience still find their way into----."

He regarded me oddly.

"Oh, wait," I said. "You're not saying that with regret...."

"Why would I say it with regret?" he asked.

It is necessary to the gist of the story that I outline how successful Grace was at the school, to indicate what she was to give up. She almost immediately established herself as the top student in most subjects; her teachers sang her praises, and one stated she was the most remarkable girl he'd ever known, and seemed to suspect she was some great spirit reincarnate; she won the lead in the school play, to raves; in her first full month, she was named "Student of the Month"; all the most popular girls, even from higher grades, would come to our flat to visit or to study, grade elevens gaining the benefit of her tutelage; she would play classical pieces for them on her piano, and some of the girls would try to conjure up the pieces of past piano lessons; some even tried to imitate her distinct, very stylish style of dress. I overheard one girl say "Grace, your mom is real beautiful." and another say "What did you expect?" Whatever Grace favoured established what was cool, for Grace has always been thoroughly cool.

And so has her older brother, Gabriel, an obvious fact that wasn't lost on one girl in particular who often visited. She was in grade eleven and was the daughter of a Saudi business magnate reaping the returns of operating in the land of the world's cheapest workforce. Her name was Noorah, and she was, by arrangement, already engaged to be married. Her fiancé had just started at university in the U.S., studying commerce (it seems as if all Muslim sons of privilege study commerce or business), and he was everything that Gabriel, who is poetic, darkly romantic, intellectual, witty, iconoclastic, and adventurous, was not, and vice versa.

Noorah had a certain sweetness that was, to that point, surviving the fact she was utterly spoiled by her wealthy family; she was a girl who was used to getting what she wanted, including, it seemed, a B.Comm boy, but she'd never before wanted anything like handsome, be-excited Gabriel. It seemed to me that she was frustrated in her undeveloped capacity to get what she wished without simply voicing it. She would, as her group of girls passed through the hallway to Grace's room, be suddenly arrested by the overwhelmingly interesting process of Gabriel adjusting one string on his guitar, and she would, naturally, be drawn, in an absent way, into the living room by her fascination. As she'd never actually been intensely interested in anything, she had to feign its facial expression; she managed a sort of quietly mournful look. Whenever the course of the visits arrived at sowaddiawannadonow, Noorah's eyes would be alert to any flicker of response in Gabriel.

Now, Grace came to find the purified atmosphere of the A.I.S. bubble stifling; she began to suspect that she'd been doing much better in the filthy thick of Bangladesh than were those in the elaborate, expensive exclusion of it. Also, she sorely missed the more demanding rigours of her private education. Among the rigours of my children's education was the necessity that any argument be presented with impeccable and compelling logic, were it to survive the critical scrutiny of three or four other sharp minds. Grace prepared arguments as airtight as A.I.S. itself for her leaving it,

141

supported by quotations from Tennyson's 'Ulysses'; she's highly skilled in debate, as some of her teachers were occasionally finding to their chagrin.

I played the devil's advocate quite extensively, but left the decision to her, in the end, after a long period of sober second thought and reflection. She informed the school that she would be leaving at the end of the year, and the guidance counsellor promptly phoned me.

"You know that I profoundly respect your educational objectives and methods with your children," he said.

"You do?" I asked. "I mean, I do?"

"But Grace is now part of a select group that is heading toward the Ivy League and all the promise that entails. I'm worried that she doesn't fully understand what she's giving up."

"Feel free to press your case to her," I said. "And I shall, too."

Her mind was made up, though, and her reasons were so strong, we allowed her to leave. Maybe the Ivy League would have to stagger along without her. Not her school friends, however, who continued to call, among them being Noorah, whose pursuit of Gabriel's attention became more overt as did his lack of sufficient response.

Grace and Gabriel were making new friends, as well, although of a very different social echelon, as they were much involved in our project in association with a large financial cooperative for poor women of several slums, providing English lessons to its members and its members' young adult offspring. This programme was to evolve into the teacher-training programme for our 'Mothers of Intention' project schools. Among those enrolled who distinguished themselves in one way or another were three particularly germane to this little story: Iqbal is a good-looking young man of easy geniality, and Nipa and Farzana are immediately noticed for their genuine beauty, although they present themselves in differing ways; Nipa's style of salwar kamees is more muted elegance, while younger Farzana's is bolder, more definite; that we can be discussing personal style in two young women of poverty is a testament to both their determination and their creativity; they both look superb all the time. Farzana's beauty had already been brokered by her parents into an advantageous engagement to a boy of a more prosperous family.

One of the great things about teaching English is that one may do it by just discussing anything. Our method, for a number of pedagogically-sound reasons we won't go into here, employs songs and the subjects that arise in them. Grace's birthday fell on one of our early lessons, so I used the opportunity to teach the class "Happy Birthday To You"©.

We were the first foreigners these young people had met, and when we began together their curiosity was tempered with a bit of wariness in most. I stated outright, in our first lesson, that we'd be making no attempt whatsoever to dispute Islam or Bangladeshi culture, but they could expect to be exposed to other ideas and customs.

Birthday celebrations were becoming common (and extravagant) among the wealthy, but were unknown among the poor. Iqbal has a progressive approach to life, and was the most worldly, or, rather, least unworldly of that first batch of students, and he apparently had a scrap of information about birthdays, for at the next lesson, with appropriate ceremony and through Iqbal's organization, Grace was presented with a slightly belated birthday gift, brightly wrapped. It was a sweet flower

143

vase, cheap by Canadian standards, but significant to our students' pooled taka. We were very moved, and our students very excited. At that point, I think, began our own, independent Amarok Society culture, which includes happy celebration of our staff's and students' birthdays. I tell you, these poor young people have a real natural talent for parties, all liquor-free and regret-free, that their wealthy, just-reserve-a-restaurant compatriots could do well to study.

At that point, too, began the friendship between Grace and Farzana; although Farzana is a few years older, it was natural that they should gravitate to each other, as their essences have so much in common: both are sublimely beautiful, intelligent, strong-willed, energetic, industrious, generous, loving and so deeply, deeply romantic in their pure hearts, Waterhouse paintings could replace their mirrors. Farzana had almost no English when she began with us, but by studious application and her quick wits, she developed it rapidly (although with her own syntax, so charming I can't quite bring myself to correct it), but their friendship didn't wait for it.

It seemed to me that poor Iqbal was coming under some stress in his life, as I'd observed that he was developing a subtle but definite nervous tic; at the beginning of each lesson, he would always set himself in one of a pair of empty seats ---- it was, apparently, his compulsive requirement that he have an empty seat beside him ---- at which point he would set his eyes on a middle-distance nothing and his head would invariably begin a very slight bobbing dip in the direction of the empty seat, and it would carry on until the lesson had started. I reported this to Gabriel after one lesson, and he said he'd noticed it, too.

Grace said, "That's odd. Nipa has a nervous tic, too. Haven't you seen it?"

"I've been preoccupied with Iqbal's," I said.

"At the start of every class, Nipa's head shakes, pauses, shakes, pauses...."

"Hmmm," I said. "Next lesson, let us compare tics."

And at the next lesson, this is what we observed: Iqbal sat down and, scrupulously looking at nothing, almost imperceptibly bobbed his head down to the empty seat beside him. Sitting in a seat across the room, beautiful Nipa, looking scrupulously at nothing, almost imperceptibly shook her head; Iqbal bobbed again; Nipa shook again; Iqbal bobbed, Nipa shook; and so it went.

"You know," I said, leaning in to Grace and Gabriel, "I don't believe Iqbal came here to learn English at all."

"French might have been more suitable," Gabriel whispered. "La langue d'amour."

Grace later consulted with her dear friend, and Farzana confided the close secret that Nipa and Iqbal were indeed desperately in love, but that both families were grimly opposed to their relationship, apparently for no other reason than that it was a love match, not arranged.

There aren't any secluded cafés in the slums, and if there had been one, Iqbal wouldn't have been able to afford it. Our offer of free English lessons in a reasonably secluded room upstairs at the financial cooperative office, hidden away from family awareness, the star-crossed lovers welcomed as heaven-sent. If Nipa couldn't bring herself to offend against propriety to the extent of actually sitting beside her beau, they could at least see and speak to each other in the context of our wide-ranging Socratic discussions. Our class was their trysting place.

If learning English wasn't their primary purpose in attending, one wouldn't have guessed it by the conscientious quality of Nipa's effort and work. She never failed to complete an assignment, and we all came to eagerly look forward to the free-thinking intelligence and humour of her essays. I don't believe Iqbal ever did an assignment, keeping his priorities in order, but he would readily volunteer to speak extemporaneously on any topic, demonstrating similar humour and independent thought.

We became very fond of them both, and thought of them as a lovely match.

We never saw or heard anything about Farzana's fiancé. I don't think she knew him at all, as he moved in higher circles.

The lower circles spun Nipa around Iqbal concentrically; lesson by lesson, she came to sit closer to the seat he always reserved for her, until her reserve was finally overcome. We took it as something of a triumph of love, the evening she casually sat beside him. They still didn't look at each other beyond furtive glances under lowered heads, but I suspect my erudition bounced off Iqbal like a rider off a reckless rickshaw that lesson.

As the English language makes such good use of phrases from Aesop's fables, we studied them between songs. The students all liked Aesop personally, or the person he may have been: they found the story of a slave rising beyond his station through sheer talent to be inspiring; but I wondered how he would fare in their assessment when I assigned the class to weigh the merits of two contradictory adages: Aesop's moral from 'The Hawk and the Nightingale', "A bird in the hand is worth two in the bush" and "Nothing ventured, nothing gained.", possibly by Chaucer. I allotted them a week to prepare their essays.

146

Before that week was through, I was laid low by dengue fever. I fell to it over a period of about ten minutes, going from feeling quite all right to believing I'd never feel well again; but Dhaka set me up neatly for it: on the day of the fever's onset, I came upon a young woman who'd just had her nose sliced off; and, then later the same afternoon, my son Azien came home with very disturbing photos of a woman hideously scarred by an acid attack; both women were, no doubt, suffering retribution for having presumed some control over their own lives, for having defied some plan or boundary established for them, crime and punishment. Then I got sick, so the days and nights of my dengue delirium were entirely haunted by swirling horror for those poor women. It was enough to have me remembering other illnesses as the good old days.

Dengue fever is mosquito-borne, and no one else in my family caught it (yet), so Grace and Gabriel took full responsibility for the evening lessons in my absence.

They were disturbed to find, at the next lesson, that Nipa didn't sit with Iqbal. Iqbal didn't look for two empty seats together, but sat dejectedly between Gabriel's pals, Rony and Johnny (formally, Md. and Md.). The sweethearts' studious avoidance of each other's eye took on a new desperate determination. Farzana, in her visit with Grace after the lesson, speculated that the burden of familial disapproval was bearing down too heavily upon the two, that they were losing heart. Grace asked what might be done, but Farzana just shook her head sadly.

Grace and Gabriel have no information regarding powerlessness; the idea of it finds no purchase in their inventive, creative minds.

In the subsequent lesson, they heard the essays comparing the two adages; I really don't know if we

147

steered the result, or if it merely reflected that those people didn't have even a bird in the hand, but the tally was:

Maybe Aesop 0
Maybe Chaucer 26

Iqbal, of course, hadn't written an essay, so G&G took the opportunity to enquire closely of him why he thought the "nothing ventured..." had gained so complete an endorsement, and they thought to paraphrase the adage with "Faint heart never won fair maiden", just for illustration, of course. They asked Nipa for further justifications for her pro-Chaucerian position.

They weren't through, though.

For the next lesson, they conducted a consideration of Gordon Lightfoot's song, 'Bitter Green'.

The class had already come to love Gordon Lightfoot. His poetry is just their stuff, picturesque, romantic and affixed to a love of the natural world around him. When they'd first discovered they could find themselves relating so closely to the heart of someone on the other side of the world who'd never even been to Bangladesh, it was a wonder to them. Their first exposure to him was when I used 'The Long River' and a terrific poem of Gabriel's to teach them something about Canadian geography, and they concluded that Canada was surely second only to Bangladesh as a cradle of poetic genius.

So they loved and trusted Lightfoot even before G&G aimed 'Bitter Green' at them. His tale of a lovely young woman wasting away for want of her one true love, of her true love, a weary stranger, arriving too late, his tears falling in the dust of the churchyard ---- well, after G&G explained what a churchyard is and its significance to the situation ---- fully achieved G&G's design. The last guitar notes still echoed soft as

148

eiderdown, and the class was hushed with grief. And as for the specific targets of this bolt, poor Nipa and Iqbal never stood a chance. The conversation to follow didn't correspond at all to an inculcated culture of arranged marriage that had overcome the longing for spontaneous love.

G&G went to the next class all set with a sung version of Yeats' 'Song of the Wandering Aengus', and if that failed, 'The Liebestod' from Wagner's 'Tristan und Isolde', which, really, would have had nothing to do with learning English, unless they meant to support the thin argument that English is a dialect of German. They had a loaded Windows Media Player, and they weren't afraid to use it. Fortunately for all concerned, such drastic measures, with their high risk of "collateral damage", were unnecessary: when the class convened, Nipa sat herself in the empty seat Iqbal had once again reserved for her.

G&G told me nothing of their programme at the time, out of pity for my weakened condition, possibly. To what degree it had steeled Iqbal's and Nipa's resolve, we can't be sure, but we know that they set the date of their wedding according to our convenience to attend.

Their families, finally facing fact, got together and arranged the match retroactively, pro forma.

Bangladeshi weddings take four days. Nipa's and Iqbal's wedding was worthy of a story of its own. What I'll record here is that the celebration of the first night was held in a large tent fitted somehow into the cramped slum, and the hundreds of guests entered in a procession along a lantern-lit passage; lining the side of the passage were perhaps two dozen women associated with the families who handed out little gifts to the guests, inexpensive tokens, such as pens, rings, sweets, even just little pieces of gold foil snipped into ornamental shapes; both Grace and Tanyss, divine in their sarees, were recruited to pass out gifts, with Tanyss positioned near the entranceway to the tent, and Grace halfway along. Standing beside Grace was her friend Farzana.

At one point, Grace asked her, none too happily, "How long will it be before I'm doing this at your wedding?"

Farzana looked at her squarely.

"I don't be marry," she said firmly.

"What do you mean?"

"I teaching poor women for Amarok Society, like you, then I going to university, like you."

"But what will your parents say?"

Farzana turned resolute eyes to her future.

"I don't be marry that boy," she said with finality. "I be lawyer for Amarok Society."

I stated outright, in our first lesson at the class that was to develop into our teacher-training programme, that we'd be making no attempt whatsoever to dispute Islam or Bangladeshi culture, but our students could expect to be exposed to other ideas and customs. However, the sheer fact of us being there, having come from wealthy Canada to teach poor Bangladesh, was, perhaps, the most emphatic other idea, and emboldened our brighter students, both in that project and in our mothers' schools in the direst slums, immediately to reappraise what might be possible in their lives. The established narrow parameters seemed inviolate no more.

Neither Grace nor Farzana might have anticipated that they were destined to find their closest counterparts from the exact opposite side of the world, were to come to stand together as life's dazzling miracles, black and white and radiant all over, in the public declaration of the new, unimagined possibility.

150

Noorah the hawk fails to figure out how to snatch a guitar-playing nightingale without first letting go of the dead-weight dead certainty already within her grasp and that keeps her earth-bound, becalmed. The organs of society promise to reward the conformist, but they're unreliable in fulfilling their promise, unless the usual wage of slavery is somehow a reward; life is much more faithful in trying to reward its explorer, but in ways the conformist could never appreciate.

There are those everywhere in the world who despise the very things we all require to survive. In my home province, there are many who have found it possible to hate trees, and bitter greens who admire trees enough, but despise any notion of human beauty; everywhere, there are those who despise or deny love; there are those who seek to thwart life's necessity to explore the new possibility: noses get sliced, acid gets thrown; but the alert human heart still risks all to respond to life's imperatives.

Grace departs the express to the success of the Ivy League; Farzana departs the express to the security of the middle class; the decisions are the same, to dare to explore the ethereal exhortation that there may be, must be, more.

And we who find ourselves as agents of their arousal must keep faith with them.

MUNNI

Munni, of All My Children....

Munni, of all my children.... her face as round, as bright and dark as the moon, Moon-i, of all my children....

It has been, since I first became a father, my contention that the doctrine of Papal infallibility is entirely dependent upon the policy of Papal celibacy: nothing lays fallibility at one's clay feet quite so incontrovertibly as fatherhood.

O, I used to seem a smartly-turned-out world-beater until I incautiously, unwittingly strayed into a wild summer foreign field and began collecting burr-babies on my sharp-creased trouser legs, began collecting little circular milk kisses on my crisp lapels and, worse, sported them as decorations better than boutonnières.

Tanyss and I first became parents over a gestation not of nine months, but of more like nine minutes, when a generous community expressed its gratitude to us in the only way available to it, by placing its best baby in Tanyss' arms and our hearts. I loved Tanyss at first sight, and never stopped, so it didn't come as a complete surprise that I should also love our beautiful tiny Azien at first sight, or that I've never stopped. And his abrupt arrival forever dispensed with any planned-parenthood conceits we might affect.

Since then, I have, without design, collected children from hither and yon. Some are also Tanyss' children, but, oddly, some are her sisters or brothers, instead. As Ruma ---- who is my daughter but Tanyss' sister ---- says, it is a confusing family, but, as I say, suitable to a confusing life.

I didn't recognize Munni as my daughter when I first met her. It wasn't until some time later that she advised me that I was her father.

Our first meeting was outside the one market that believed it was catering to the tastes of the very small international population of this teeming tangle of a South Asian city. She, along with a number of her colleagues, mainly other women and several dirty children, was begging outside the market's doors, hoping to arouse pity in the pit-eyed, overfed foreigners while eluding the frequent attacks of baton-brandishing security guards. The guards beat women and children alike with grim determination, and the beggars ebb and flow. (I've been asked why the people of this country continue to live in coastal areas so susceptible to cyclones and tidal waves, why they live and plant on silt islands the mighty rivers might erode away in a night. The answer is the same as why these beggars always return to the spot from which they've just been brutally driven: they have no choice.)

She was holding a year-old boy on her hip who was naked but for a thin string tied around his waist and a black smudge on his forehead to ward off evil spirits, and she manoeuvred herself to block my path. She was wearing a cheap cotton saree, and was unusually tall in a land of small, often stunted, people, and she was quite dark, reed-slender, and unusually beautiful, her face lively, and eyes sparkling, with intelligence. I estimated her age to be early-twenties, and I liked her right away.

"Khub balo babu," I said to her, complimenting her on the handsome little fellow.

"Nah balo babu, boss," she said with an exaggerated concern. "Babu very, very problem, boss, very, very problem."

Some beggars borrow babies from other women, for the occupational advantage a baby confers, and the baby is invariably very, very problem. 'V' isn't in the Bangla repertoire, so it's pronounced "berry, berry problem", leading Gabriel to suggest "We're in a jam."

154

Some beggars dope their babies to make them appear ill, some maintain their babies in genuine illness for the greater pity that arouses; in one example, I was approached by a young man whose baby was afflicted with a terrible skin condition that appeared to me to be treatable, so I gave him an amount of money and exhorted him to get medical attention. When he chased me again a few days later, it was clear that he'd sought no treatment, just as clear as the fact that he never would; I told him I would take him and his baby to a clinic, but he declined; his baby's suffering was his most valuable asset.

Munni's baby was clearly her own, and she would never, I came to know, cause her baby distress. However, she did undertake to press his head down to her shoulder, while shaking her own with worry she hoped was infectious.

"Babu very, very problem, boss."

"Nah babu very problem," I said. "Babu khub balo."

She opened her mouth to a slot and cast her eyes to some indeterminate distance off my shoulder, to show that she herself was sick with worry. (When, much later, I was to see her truly sick with worry, her expression was nothing like that.)

But the babu was most unprofessional, insisted on raising his head and smiling at me with his mother's black pearl sparkle in miniature.

He was so delightful, and his mother's protests of his malaise so absurd in contrast, I began laughing. She regarded me with concern for my heartlessness for a brief moment, then looked to her beaming baby boy, and it was my laughter that proved to be the most contagious in the circumstance. The baby laughed and giggled, and then she laughed with us, with happy abandon, her smile revealing the red-orange stains of betel-chew addiction on the edges of her teeth.

Thereafter, whenever she saw me, she didn't bother with any pitiable postures, but greeted me with wide smiles and laughter; something in her manner always suggested that we were still sharing an inside joke. Her begging sorority quit being pathetic, too, and would approach me with the happiness that is much more in their true nature. Whether or not I gave them money had no effect on their demeanour. Any time one of them presented an aspect of unhappiness or illness, I could know it was genuine.

It became apparent that Munni was the dominant personality of the group, and had assumed a sort of leadership. Within my family, we came to refer to her as the Beggar Queen.

She clarified our relationship with typical confidence and logic one day when Gabriel and I came upon her. She pointed to Gabriel and asked me, "Babu?"

"Yes, my baby," I said, just what every seventeen-year-old son likes to hear.

She held her finger up in an instructional manner to gain Gabriel's attention, then used it to point from Gabriel to me. "Father," she said.

"Yes," Gabriel admitted.

She pointed to herself and then to me, and said with certainty, "Father."

Gabriel accepted this in the way that misery loves company.

She pointed from herself again, and then to Gabriel, saying "Bhai", brother, just to further clarify, and then she widened her eyes in the happy wonder of it all. She chooses bhais well, I'd say, for Gabriel is quite unflappable and is the soul of generosity, so he merely smiled and nodded.

156

From then on, she treated the matter as settled. Whenever I'd encounter her, she would cry "Father!", run to me and take my arm, apparently delight in my company, and flagrantly revel in the protection I provided from the excesses of the security guards, and enjoy the protection she provided from the excessive intrusions of her colleagues; when, every now and then, another beggar ventured to call me 'Father', Munni would rebuke her sharply, eyes hot, insist that I was her father only, and that the others should regard me as 'boss'. Somehow, we came to be able to visit and talk above and around the language barrier. Somehow, we came to understand and know each other. She told me that she was a widow, and that she lived in an extensive slum I could see across a polluted man-made lake that separated my upscale neighbourhood from her desperately poor one, that she had three children, Rabi, the baby boy, and two daughters aged five and eight. (She was unusual for someone of her bottom-rung social level in that she readily knew the exact ages of her children; birthday celebrations are unknown to them; Wahid, our rickshaw wallah, could only make vague guesses as to the age of his two young daughters, and couldn't quite understand why we would ask such a difficult and pointless question.) In this society, to be widowed is another unmitigated disaster in a land of unmitigated disasters ---- natural, social, political ---- in a life that is strictly hand-to-mouth, the hand is always one slip from being empty, and options as empty a concept, that police and guard clubbings can be for the crime of being a widow.

Tanyss and I once lived with people of the Carrier First Nation, a disjunct tribe of the northern Dené; They were named Carrier because, historically, widows were required to carry the bones of their dead husbands in a

157

pouch on their backs; but before that, they were to burn the flesh from the bones by placing the corpse on a fire, and to lie down on it to keep it flat through the burning; it was usual that the widows were badly burned; many, it is said, preferred to kill themselves first. In South Asia, a woman surviving the death of her husband can be regarded as a fate worse than death, too. Many religions and customs allow dark suspicions about the potency of women, and strict measures to contain it, and institutional punitive reactions against a woman daring to confront the necessities of surviving a husband can't be too surprising.

Munni is nothing if not potent, and exceptionally tough. Official thugs with clubs can never make her cry; they probably think nothing can make her cry, just laugh and spit fire, for they don't know the secret of how to do it; but I do; I know the route to her tender heart. She sheds tears over me all the time.

Such as:

Tanyss and I would look across the sewage lake at the rickety slum hive of bamboo and tin shacks. We'd see the children splashing and playing in the foul water.

We knew that there were thousands of children within the slum without a hope of an education that could, possibly, save them from their abject circumstances. A foreigner, or even a member of a higher social echelon, is not at liberty to waltz into such a slum unbidden, it is dangerous and defensive, not that outsiders are generally known to wish to venture within; this is a strictly hierarchical society, defying the egalitarian prescriptions of the country's religion and constitution. But just as Munni was beaten for daring to trespass into the world of the small upper middle-class, so the reverse might be expected.

We'd tried, elsewhere, to address the problem of the millions of uneducated children by starting little schools for them, and had seen our efforts thwarted by various threats of everything chaotic ---- natural, social, political ---- for instance, the panic after the paroxysm of extremism, political masquerading and raiding as religious, of four hundred bombs exploding across the country within thirty minutes of each other. So we'd arrived at another design to reach the children, one we felt was more firmly grounded, sustainable and had the promise of scales of multiplication, through their mothers, by teaching their mothers to be neighbourhood teachers. We'd already heard from other agencies that our plan was an inspired, splendid one that none of them would touch with a ten-mile pole because of the inherent impossible difficulties of teaching illiterate slum women to be teachers. And so Tanyss and I would look across at the slum and wonder how we'd ever get in to try to help dear little Rabi and his like.

I'd broached the subject a couple of times to my new daughter and her cohorts, of teaching them to read and write in both their own language and in English, the language of privilege and success here, and arithmetic, so they could teach their children, and the reaction had always been negative. Literacy was for others, they clearly believed, not for them, as though it were one burden, at least, they could choose to escape; "Nah reading," Munni would say firmly on behalf of all the doubtful faces on shaking heads.

One day, Tanyss and I resolved that I'd remonstrate with Munni once more, try to convince her of her duty to the children. Munni was pivotal to our effort, we knew: if we could enrol Munni, other mothers would follow her. What I also wanted of her that day was to take me into the slum, to scout for possible locations for a school. As I approached the market, I wondered how I might approach the topic, as well.

Fate intervened in its typical way, that is, in the way that was to cost us unimagined amounts of effort, emotion, time and money.

Munni was indeed outside the market on that day, but it wasn't to beg. She was hoping to find me. And the first thing she gasped out as she raced to me was "Father, come to my house!"

Her anxiety was very plain. I don't suppose it's actually possible for Munni to be pale, but somehow she imparted that impression.

I don't recall if she awaited my consent before waving for a passing rickshaw. I do remember that she made no attempt to explain anything to me as we rode toward the slum.

And I remember the walk into the slum along a pathway of soft red Bangladeshi bricks set into the ochre-grey clay. To our right was a steep bank down to the lake. We walked past a little tea stall, where all the lean young men sipping there turned on the benches to watch me under lowered brows, past a few little market stalls, and then on past the first of the mean little shanties of bamboo and corrugated tin, with women on their haunches before clay ovens staring up through their smoke, alarmed by the sight of me, and children gaping wide-eyed from dark doorways. We stepped around a couple of goats and a duck with ducklings, a few hens, but it was a dog that gave voice, I suspect, to the general reaction to my appearance there: it barked furiously at me, and growled and snarled, and circled around me; Munni, nerves taut, grabbed a stick from the dirt and chased after the dog, whipping at it savagely, and I had the impression her message was being generally broadcast. She wheeled back to me and took my hand, and threw her wild glare all about us.

She led me into a long, very narrow passage of bamboo poles rather sparsely and unevenly placed lengthwise, that rose sharply between two ranks of hovels. We had to squeeze past some of the bulging, collapsing tin walls. I could see, looking down between the poles beneath our feet, that we were walking quite high above a bog, that that section of the slum dwellings was mounted on bamboo stilts, precariously, I felt. As we passed open doorways of the dark little rooms, people on little plank cots sat up suddenly, startled and concerned.

Munni led me by the hand through a door, into her tiny home. A raised bed occupied most of the space, and on it lay Munni's eight-year old daughter, beautiful, thin, shaven-headed, Munni in miniature, unmoving, dressed in a pair of old shorts and a threadbare sweater; her large black eyes followed me as I entered, but with a dull resignation that told a terrible tale. There was no doubt in my mind that she was dying.

I sat down beside her and put my hand on her forehead.

"How long has she been sick?" I asked. "How many days?"

Munni held up four fingers.

"What is her name?"

"Hira."

Suspended from the bamboo roof poles were four or five small plastic mesh bags. Munni brought one down and pulled from it a piece of paper, which she handed to me. It was from the nearest medical clinic, which was in another very poor neighbourhood a few miles away. Apparently Munni had somehow scraped together enough to take Hira to be seen there. Most of the printing on the paper was in Bangla, but the diagnosis and recommendation for treatment were scrawled in English; it was no surprise: typhoid.

Typhoid can be readily responsive to a course of antibiotics, but, untreated, it can cripple or kill. People whose everyday diet is inadequate amounts of rice and lentils are constitutionally unequipped to mount much of a battle against it. The cost of treatment was about $60, but, for Munni's resources, might have been a million dollars.

It's hard for a Canadian to imagine what it's like to be a parent standing with her child in a clinic, being told "All you need to restore your child is right there, behind that dispensary wicket, but you'll never have the money for it, so take your child home to die." To the Canadian sensibility, it is monstrous. What is a child's life worth? There's no answer to that rhetorical question in Canada; in Bangladesh, for most children, the question isn't rhetorical, and its answer is something less than $60.

I looked from the page to the listless little girl, then to her mother, who stood motionless, breathless, I think, staring at me in dread apprehension of the next step, the last desperate hope. I had a flash in my mind of her earlier, waiting on the street, searching the distance for whether I might be coming along. She was terrified of the power I possessed.

"Rickshaw," I said.

Munni was gone like a shot.

I gathered up the little girl as nothing upon my arms. Her bald head sank against my shirt.

As I was negotiating the bamboo walkway, people came to their doorways and watched. One young man nodded to me with fervour. An older woman said, most seriously, "Yes, sir, yes, sir."

By the time I reached the brick footpath, I was leading a lengthy, joyless parade of consternation. Alas, it was not for the last time that I was.

Munni had found a rickshaw, which waited at the end of the path, and she raced back to meet us.

"Father," she said, motioning that she would carry Hira, as though the little soul could be a burden to anyone.

"Nah," I said, but Munni is stubborn and insistent. She might have felt it was beneath my dignity to carry her, but, just as likely, she might have badly needed something more to do.

Munni and I sat side by side on the little seat of the rickshaw, with Hira on her mother's lap. Several times during our wild, careening ride to the clinic, mainly on a major thoroughfare intermingling with thundering dilapidated buses and swerving trucks and vans and three-wheeler taxis as though we travelled a braid in Satan's tail, Munni pressed her leg hard against mine, quite deliberately. It might have been in fear of the hellish traffic, but I thought at the time that she was convincing herself that I was actually there.

We turned down a heaving side road and stopped before a small concrete apartment building. The clinic occupied the building's first floor. As everywhere in the most densely-populated city in the world, in the most densely-populated country, the waiting area of the clinic was crowded with people of obvious poverty. The Queen stepping into a grocery to shoplift a tin of sardines would have created less stir and amazement than I did coming into the clinic.

There were a few ranks of moulded plastic seats, and Munni made for them immediately, barking at men sitting in two of them in the front row. They seemed more than willing to vacate them for us, and so did several others in the vicinity, who instantly cleared out to watch us from an intent, indiscreet distance. I sat down and Munni deposited Hira's little stick figure in my lap, and went in search of whomever was in charge, taking the clinical paper with her.

Within a short time, she was back, sitting beside me, holding Hira. People nearby shot sharp questions at her. Her reply, that I was her father, did nothing whatsoever to answer their confusion.

A woman in a white uniform came to us and told me, sorry for late, sir, sorry you sit here, sorry, and that the clinic administrator was on his way downstairs to meet me, and would I please await him in his office? I told her that I would be pleased to wait in the office, and that I wished Hira's treatment to begin without delay. Munni hadn't understood this exchange, and she gripped my arm urgently as I stood, but the woman spoke to her.

I was seated in a small office, at a little metal desk. The administrator soon joined me, introducing himself with typical courtesy and welcome. He was professionally attired, in dress shirt and tie. He asked me my homeland, and nodded with real interest when I said it was Canada.

"May I ask, sir," he said as he sat behind the desk, "are you with a medical relief agency?"

I told him that I was with a small educational agency.

"So this matter with the little girl," he asked, "is an act of impromptu charity?"

"It's an act of finding the alternative, inaction, intolerable," I said.

"I see," he said seriously. He went on to tell me how desperately in financial need his clinic was, and asked if it were possible that I knew of Canadian funding opportunities for it.

I told him honestly that we were very worried about our own funding, that Canadians are arguably the most well-meaning, well-wishing people in the world, but such penny-pinchers our thumbprints are little profiles of the Queen; I told him that when it came to charitable donation, Canadians ranked just about bottom of the developed world, that even borderline developed countries like Portugal and Spain outdo us in per capita donation, and that Scandinavia and the U.S. absolutely eclipse us. He was shocked by this, had assumed that a rich country like Canada was numbered among the international powerhouses.

"Yes," I said. "Canadians, in self-assessment, usually make that same mistake. We have all the potential to be big fish, but we choose to be minnows with big fish stories."

Still, he asked as he gave me his card, could I please think of the clinic if any opportunities arose?

"Well, actually, you know," I said, "I was rather hoping you could do something about reducing the cost of the little girl's treatment. I don't have enough taka with me to pay for it. I only have about half of it."

He appeared deeply concerned, shaking his head. Every cost is negotiable in Dhaka, and I had honed, through trial but mainly error, my skills to a keenness that could leave the most practiced merchant shaking his head in admiration, but this administrator would have none of it. The course of treatment was to continue for eight days, with one injection per day, but he insisted that the entire course must be paid for up front. After much polite back and forth, during which he even withstood my most effective protracted periods of silence, the best that I could wrangle from him was an agreement that I could pay for half the course of treatment that day and pay the remainder the next day.

He escorted me out to the dispensary, where he explained our arrangement to the two men behind the wicket. I paid and was given the doses, then went back to Munni and Hira. In a short time, the woman in white came again, and she and Munni took Hira to receive the first injection.

Munni came out of the examination room in another moment.

She stood in the middle of the waiting area, a bit in front of where I was sitting, and looked about herself with a sudden expression of bewildered wonder. In an instant, that strength and urgent tension that had kept her upright through her ordeal broke, and she collapsed, falling forward to clutch at my knees, to bury her face in my lap, to sob into me.

"Father! Father!" she cried over and over.

I stroked her head as the people surrounding us looked on. There's no privacy in Dhaka. Expressions of joy and grief, fury and relief, a daughter pouring four days of the unthinkable inevitable into her father's lap are all public spectacles and are treated as such. No one averts his eyes, because it's as natural to watch as they are to do. Maybe some of those watching started to wonder if I really might be her father, after all.

Hira was to return to the clinic everyday at the same time for her injections.

As Munni carried her back along the brick path leading into the slum, I was able to regard it more calmly and thoroughly. Set into the middle of the pathway was a small brick structure; it concealed the single toilet for the entire extensive slum, a concrete ground-level platform with an oval hole in it. There was, much further along, the slum's single hand pump providing water, water of dangerous properties.

166

There were little branch paths winding down the bank to the lake, to muddy landings from which people took their daily baths. Personal cleanliness is very important in BD, although this seemed to be more an exchange of toxins. There were several children splashing in the effluence as we went by.

We came upon the same dog, and once again it barked furiously at me, but no longer was it the growl of the community. A man nearby chased it with a growl of his own, and then he smiled at me apologetically. All along, people acknowledged me with a new openness and acceptance.

And all along were children and children, babes in arms, darling smiling girls, daring smart-alec boys marching along beside me and shaking my hand in mock ceremony, acting as if, just as with boys everywhere, they themselves had invented daring smart-alecism in boys.

When we had delivered little Hira to the hard bed in Munni's room, Munni insisted that I wait while she fetched me a cup of tea from the stall. While men, women and children crowded at the doorway, I sat beside Hira, and she watched me, her dark eyes slowly closing and opening, as I looked about the room.

I was to come to know that these hovels were all illegal, gripping onto what was simply a strip of raised ground between the lake on one side and the bog on the other, and were under threat at any time from government bulldozers, and dire rumours of their imminent destruction circulated daily through its complex of narrow bamboo passageways. That they were illegal didn't mean they were unclaimed in terms of ownership, and Munni had to pay a "manageress" a rent of $20 per month. From the roof hung an electrical cord and light bulb, which Munni was permitted by rental condition to turn on for one hour per day. Beside the bed was a little table, and along the wall opposite to the bed was a narrow sort of counter holding a small paper bag of rice, a little bottle of mustard oil, and two or three other little bags. On a shelf below it were a couple of plastic glasses, a couple of plastic plates, a few cooking implements and a couple of cheap, charred aluminum vessels. The floor, what little of it I could see, was of old wooden planks, cracked and uneven, and widely spaced, so that I could see ripples of light reflecting from the bog ten feet below.

It turned out that there were five people living in this room, Munni and her three children, and Roxanna, Munni's younger sister, whom I was about to meet. At the end of the bed was a cotton curtain, behind which another family of six lived. Some of the other little rooms had eight or nine people living in them.

Munni pushed her way through the crowd at the door to present me with a glass half-full of tea; it's the latest thing at tea stalls here to brew a very strong tea, and then add a spoonful of instant coffee to it, and then cut its bite with a lot of sugar and coffee whitener. Until it was explained to us, Tanyss and I had quite a time trying to identify it, whenever hospitable shopkeepers would insist we take some: it's coffee ... no wait, it's tea... no....

Roxanna came in. I would never have identified her as Munni's sister. She was very pretty, like Munni, but shy and subdued, very self-possessed. Where Munni's intelligence crackled in her eyes, Roxanna's seemed thoughtful and rational.

Munni introduced us, Roxanna my apa, Father.

"Hello, Father," Roxanna said.

I looked at Hira, and then at the little children at the door.

"Yes, I am your father," I said.

My two daughters nodded.

168

"What I want to know is," I said, "are my daughters going to obey their father?"

"Yes, Father," they nodded solemnly.

"Good," I said. "As soon as Hira is well again, my daughters and I are going to begin a school for mothers in this room."

"School...," said Munni.

"For mothers," I said.

"My house...."

"Yes."

They looked at each other. But they know how to be good daughters.

"Yes, Father," they said.

Hira's health improved impressively, and within a few days she'd progressed from the bottled water we'd supplied to a sort of rice milk Munni concocted. I went with them to the clinic for Hira's daily injection.

In the room in which she was to receive it, a little girl was being treated with a steam inhaler. I asked the nurse there if it was for asthma; she said yes; I asked if they were seeing more cases as the city's atmosphere became ever more besmirched; she said it was an epidemic.

Munni couldn't bear to see her daughter being injected. It was a long process, of a slow injection into a little tube inserted into the back of her hand. Munni gripped my hand throughout, tightly enough that it was possible I was suffering more than Hira, and turned her face into my shoulder until it was over. Hira, on the other hand, so to speak, observed the procedure stoically.

I rode only part way home with them on the rickshaw, and when I took my leave of them, as I looked at Hira leaning weakly into her mother but smiling at me, I was rather overcome by her little girl's courage, and impulsively I kissed her cheek. It wasn't meant as a reward, merely as my self-expression. It's most unlikely she'd ever been kissed before, but forever thereafter, whenever I encounter her, she insists that I must give and receive a kiss.

Now all my daughters and granddaughters expect a kiss. It's another epidemic.

At one time, my daughter Roxanna became betrothed to be my second wife, by a design of the women of our school. It was considered quite inconsequential that I didn't happen to know of the arrangement any more than Tanyss did. So Munni would have been my daughter and my sister-in-law, and Hira would have been my granddaughter and niece. Ours is, as my daughter Ruma noted, a confusing family, but I didn't think it should be quite that confusing.

O, but I know what makes my daughter Munni cry. Such as:

One of the mothers who attended our school right from the outset was a beggar named Morium. When she began, she had no idea how to hold a pencil; she had no idea which end of the pencil went to the page. When she first began to try to copy the mark presented on the whiteboard, she held her paper unsupported up before her eyes and tried to stab it with her pencil point. Copying 'M' for Morium might result in a skewed '←'. However, she endured utter confusion, and possibly embarrassment, for the sake of becoming able to teach her three children, one of whom was just a baby.

When Tanyss and I were fixing up schools in remote aboriginal communities in Canada, one of the first things we would do was establish cooperative daycare centres to allow teenage mothers to continue their

170

education. There's no question of anything like that in our slum schools, however. Any women with children under the age of about three will, just as a matter of course, bring them. Morium always brought her baby girl, and when not feeding her beneath her shawl, she would lay the baby down on the woven palm mats that, except for the little plastic stool for Tanyss or me, constitute the entirety of our school furniture. The baby would kick and gurgle the way all babies do.

Something about my appearance really appealed to the baby, and whenever she became unhappy, Morium would hold her up so she could see me, and soon she would be beaming. Anytime she became too restive, hands would pass her to my lap, where she would sit and gum my hand happily.

Their plans regarding Roxanna and me having been thwarted, the women soon settled, to their constant amusement, that this baby was determined to become my next wife, and they would refer to her as 'Tanyss' rival' to unfailing hilarity.

She really was the sweetest baby, and her eyes sparkled with internal light.

The reaction of the husbands to their wives attendance at our schools has been mixed. For the most part it has been quite good, sometimes very good, where the husband makes time to allow his wife to do extra study, where he boasts of her accomplishment, "My wife stood third in her exam!" Men and boys have always gathered at the doors and windows (if there is a window) of our schools to look in on the lessons for which they don't qualify. But at our first school, at Munni's house until I began to worry that her plank floor above the bog was going to collapse under the weight of all the women cramming into it, when we rented a nearby room on solid clay (solid until the floods come), some of the husbands were perturbed. Some threatened their wives, some beat them, when they attended our school.

One day, Morium was unusually quiet through the class, and she held a rag to her eye. At one point, I led her to the doorway, to look at her eye in the light. Her eyelid was perforated right through, and her eye beneath it damaged. Weeping, she explained that her husband, an affable-seeming fellow I knew, had beaten her with a stick because she insisted on coming to school.

By some fluke, the wound wasn't yet infected, and I dressed it with the medical kit I'd soon learned we had to have in each school.

That was maybe the fourth such incident in recent days, and I'd had enough.

Bangladesh has lately had a new government elected, one for which we have high hopes; the corrupted and discredited previous regime had, amongst numerous sins, undertaken a programme to deal with the backlog of criminal cases before the courts by the expedient of "extra-judicial executions" which the government called "Operation Clean-Heart". At first it was the army that was charged with the job of dispensing by bullet or beating any un-arrested, untried undesirables, but then the programme was assigned to the elite police force. This force was originally created because the regular force was deemed to be irredeemably corrupt. It was formed from the best, and possibly cleanest, members of the regular police. They were named the Rapid Action Battalion, or RAB, and they were a striking bunch in more ways than one, too, men and women dressed head-to-toe in black, with black bandanas tied over their heads and black sunglasses.

It so happens that my sons Azien and Gabriel and I are very often dressed at least neck-to-ankle in black, too (we don't wear hats and we wear sandals in BD). To be taken seriously in a concrete world like Dhaka, one must attend to one's appearance, as both we and the elite police force understood, and our normal attire is black suits, often with black shirts and ties.

The day after discovering Morium's injury, Azien and Gabriel, in their black suits, accompanied me to the school, and we took my Bangladeshi daughter, Ruma, who is our administrative officer, along with us, too, to serve as translator so that I was completely understood.

When the class was assembled, I stood at the front of the room, flanked by my impressive sons.

"I have a message for you to give to your husbands," I said. "Tell your husbands that Amarok Society Women's Schools protect their students. Tell them that the RAB will do as we say. Tell them that if any husband beats, threatens, or prevents the attendance of a student of ours ever again, we will send in the RAB to take him away and kill him."

Ruma turned to me, eyes wide with surprise.

"Really, Dad?"

"Translate that for them, please, dear."

With some hesitation, Ruma translated. She reported to me "I told them you would send the RAB in to arrest him."

"But, dear, I didn't say 'arrest'."

"It makes no difference, Dad," she said. "No one in this slum who's arrested by the RAB ever comes back. Everyone knows that."

I assume that those women who needed to relayed my message. I know that the beatings stopped immediately and haven't recurred.

That wasn't the worst with Morium, however.

Some weeks later, she again seemed unhappy and distracted through the day's lessons, and at the end of the class, she made no move to leave. It was usual for me to give an extended lesson to Roxanna and another bright woman, Rubina, both of whom we'd hired to provide additional help in our school at night, for anyone who wanted to come. Most of our mothers attended. Morium continued to stand by the door as I started the special lesson, until I asked her if something were wrong.

"Father," she said (she calls me Father when Munni isn't in earshot), "apa babu. Come."

Science has no explanation for the indisputable event of the telephone ring sounding different for the call reporting disaster, or how the word 'come' could suddenly squeeze a heart with dread. Roxanna and Rubina heard it, too, closed their notebooks and stood.

"Your sister's baby?" I asked, dry of mouth.

She nodded. "Apa house. Come."

"Yes, I'll come."

She led the way. In a moment, Munni was walking with us. She took us to a hovel at the very far end of the extensive slum. More than a hundred people were gathered outside, turned to watch for our arrival, a passage through them to the door already cleared.

"This is very bad," I said aloud.

Morium stopped outside, but Munni came in with me. There were another dozen people inside the little room, crowded around the one bed.

On the bed, lying on his back, was a little boy of about eight years. He was dressed in a clean, collared shirt and neat silver-brown slacks. On another day, he might well have been a cocky, daring re-originator of smart-alecism.

I went and sat down beside him.

The first terrible indication was that he gave absolutely no reaction to the simple extraordinary fact of me being there, sitting beside him.

174

His breathing was very rapid, shallow and raspy. His brow was wet with perspiration, but not particularly hot.

"Hello," I said to him. There was no reaction.

I passed my finger back and forth before his eyes. His eyes didn't follow it. I slowly put my finger toward his eye, closer and closer, until it was all but touching his pupil. He didn't blink.

With Munni's assistance, I managed to ascertain that, three days earlier, he had been playing on the rooves of the shanties and had fallen to the ground.

"Where was he hurt?" I asked, patting my head, arms and chest, and Munni asked in translation.

He'd complained of being hurt all over. He'd cried all day, and then he'd become worse and worse.

I took a pen from my jacket pocket, and ran its end, hard, along the sole of his bare foot. His toes should have curled downward reflexively, even if he were unconscious. His foot didn't react at all.

I lifted the little fellow into my arms, and looked at the anxious faces around the dark room, at his weeping, aging parents, for whom he must have seemed Allah's overdue reward. I spied Morium's husband, a handsome, long-haired reformed wife-beater, by the door.

"Your rickshaw!" I said to him.

He nodded, and dashed away.

A rickshaw is too wide to pass between the impacted little hovels throughout the whole slum, so we had a long way to walk. Once again, I was leading a perverted poverty parade.

My granddaughter Hira, by then in good health and growing her hair, joined her mother and me by the time our miserable throng reached the rickshaw of Morium's husband. With Munni holding Hira and me holding the little boy, we took off, and others chased behind on foot.

On the winding narrow side streets between the tiny shops, the midday traffic became impassable with pedestrians, other rickshaws and even a lunatic in a small truck hopelessly attempting to make a delivery.

This was more than take-charge Munni could bear, and she jumped down from the rickshaw and raced ahead, probably to pull rickshaws from the way, maybe to pull little trucks. Hira became our siren, her high pitch shrilly ordering surprised wallahs and walkers out of our way. She's the very spit of her mother.

Finally, we reached the main street, and there was Munni like a maddened traffic cop, risking her life to rush out to hold up raging buses and crazed cabs so that we could pass. She leapt into the rickshaw as we came by her, and Hira continued to emit orders and directions to all around us.

When we finally reached that same clinic of our earlier success, Morium's husband dismounted and took the little form from me, ran into the clinic. Munni and Hira ran after him.

I had lost all sense of urgency somewhere back on the main street as the anonymous insane pursuit of desperate mock-life careered about our fragile, defenceless contraption. I climbed down from the rickshaw and went into the clinic. Through the open door of the examination room, I could see the little boy's form laid out on the table. The seats in the waiting area were empty, for the most part, as people left them to investigate more closely what gave the appearance of being a genuine emergency. I sat in a seat at the front, possibly the seat I'd taken before.

I saw a doctor, with a stethoscope around her neck, walk into the examination room, pulling the door closed behind her.

I thought of how, as a lesson for our teacher training students, we'd played an old song entitled "Where Do the Children Play?", and then discussed the situation of this unbelievably congested, unbelievably poor city, how I've watched children trying to play cricket on rickety rooftops with bats of broken sticks and balls of bits of plastic bottles because there is nowhere else and no other way to do it, and our students contributed their own several illustrations. Aren't little children supposed to play? We'd listened to the song a second time, and the students, young men and women alike, were moved to tears. Gabriel had said afterward that he'd never imagined the song so literally or appropriately interpreted.

I pictured the doctor undoing the buttons of the neat collared shirt, and placing the stethoscope on the small still chest. I wondered if his eyes were still opened on nothing, gazing undeceived at a slum child's future.

In a moment, Munni burst through the door of the examination room, closely followed by Hira. They ran to me, and Munni managed to gasp out "Dead body!" before, once again, throwing herself down at my feet to cry and cry into my lap, with wailing little Hira diving in beside her.

The doctor left the room and went away. Morium's husband, ashen, carried the little corpse out to his rickshaw. There was no registration of the boy's death, any more than there'd ever been a registration of his birth, or a registration at a school. Those are vital statistics, and all the evidence in the whole world said there was nothing vital about the little fellow's life. There would be no autopsy to discover the cause of death; everyone already knew the cause of death; in its essence, it's always the same.

The Canadian core of our confusing family is of runners: Azien gathers the law of inertia and uses it to streak as though he need never stop, Gabriel is a golden flash, his blond hair winging out behind him, Grace could race right up an Olympic podium if that end ever became a priority to her; even young Alastair accepts that running is what a Munro does. Tanyss and I run as an act of finding the alternative, inaction, intolerable. Running in Dhaka is difficult, for even if one gets out early enough in the morning that the streets aren't totally clogged, the streets themselves are so uneven and rough, one can never reckon what the next footfall will bring; and then there's the problem of the air pollution. Where do the parents run? We run on the fancy treadmills at the exercise room of the Canadian Club. The treadmills used to face a window, beyond which was the club swimming pool. I used to be almost able to convince myself that the pool was a glimpse of Yellowhead Lake in the Rockies, just a fast-paced hour ahead of me, and that I was running to kneel at it and take a long drink.

Some wives of Canadian officials successfully pressed to have the running machines moved and a television mounted in front of them, so they could watch Asian rebroadcasts of American programmes in which small clean families in huge clean homes wrestle over tiny problems, most of which would be instantly solved if one member stopped being a complete jerk. Tanyss and I were ruined for such programmes years ago, and we've inflicted the same disability on our children. Or it might be a hard-hitting weekly story of a gruff but good-hearted doctor who brings the investment of medical millennia and multimillions to focus on the illness of a sweet child. Maybe at the end, he holds the child on his knee as she is giggling and grateful, not weeping and wailing as if her heart will never heal. Or maybe, and here's the hard-hitting part, at the end he stares out over the ocean in front of his huge clean beach house, clenching his jaw muscles and wondering "Why?"

As for us, we are spared the agonizing question, for we always know why. The malicious hands of poverty and ignorance are at play behind every dreadful thing we encounter here. We believe we can, painstakingly, frustratingly, educate people out of reproducing like rabbits, educate them out of wife-beatings, out of security guard beatings, out of typhoid, out of nowhere for the children to play but ramshackle rooves, out of chronic malnutrition; if we were to find that mattress under which Canadian wealth is secretly stashed, we wouldn't pass money on to a clinic that can only react, we would use it ourselves to pro-act, to force the clinic to near-obviation. However, lately, on my runs, as I close my mind to the ABC drivel of the television, and even the a-b-c travails of our schools, as I try to conjure an image of Yellowhead Lake's cold pellucid waters, I am arrested mid-stride by two agonizing questions of my own; I don't know why I keep returning to that little boy, it's not as though he's the only tragic thing we've seen, but I'm held up by: what if Morium hadn't waited until the very end of the lesson of the third day to intone the chilling word 'come'? and why was the boy dressed in those clothes, the button-up, collared shirt, the creased slacks? The attire of such a boy is a pair of cheap shorts and maybe a t-shirt. Where did they get those smart clothes, and why did they put them on his limp limbs, as they awaited the arrival of their last and only hope, which I was? Did they do it out of pride, or to indicate respect for me; or did they do it to try to convince me that his life was worth saving?

The parents invited Tanyss and me, several times, to travel to their home village for a rite finally marking the boy's slipping away from us, but we were too busy with those still clinging to life.

Hira attends our first school for mothers, now named, by the mothers, 'Tanyss Women's School'. It was natural that she should begin to, as the first school was in her home; when we had to move, she moved with us. She's as bright as a new dime, as intelligent as her mother, absorbs her lessons hungrily. Munni excels in school, and teaches little Rabi all she learns. He will grow up thinking it only natural that girls and women should be educated; he will fully understand what a benefit it is for all.

In this culture of poverty, at the frequent events of tragedy, it is required that men stand, stolid, strong, while the women of their family throw themselves upon them, grab at them, writhe in anguish against them, expressing every fluid ounce of their grief. Women don't get the better of most deals here, but they get the better of that one. Tough Munni needed a father upon whom to lament, and she chose me.

Sometimes she'll make me wait while she changes into her good saree, as daughters make fathers wait, and then I'll escort her along the lake's warm, fetid waters, with her brown hand in the crook of my arm. It's a sort of promenade for her, I think, an eastern parade; she'll tell me that she is surely my daughter, because we're both so well-dressed, both so tall. (I become tall on the flight to Bangladesh; it's a deft trick British Airways and I perform together.); she has stood feeding me bananas and squirts of suspect milk from a plastic pouch; at such times, she is happiness itself. But I know what makes her cry.

180

In my mind, my children are the shining promise of the world, its jewels beyond value, and every day they find new ways to convince me that I'm right.

But Munni, Moon-i, of all my children, is the dark giving way to the light giving way to the dark. She takes me by the hand and leads me again into the extreme realm of my terrifying, terrifying power, and my terrifying limitations.

RASHIDA
PEDDLING HER
WARE

The Price Everything Has

Tanyss Madam is beautiful," said Amena amid the close-quarters crowd in the sweltering heat of our slum classroom one morning.

"Yes, she certainly is," I said. "And so are you, Amena."

I wasn't saying so out of kindness, either. She is a beggar of about thirty years old who can't wholly conceal her sprightly swagger and zesty wit even as she feigns suffering for stone-faced foreigners; her brilliant smile and the sparkle in her black eyes are but an instant away at most. When she begs, she tells a joke, fate's bitter, ironic joke on herself and on those to whom she applies, and she can barely contain her knowing laughter. Her cheap saree she selected for flair and style, vivid orange and yellow. And she really is beautiful.

When Amena tells me a tale of woe, of herself or of one of her four children, I know it's the truth; and she has plenty of woes, as do all of the women in our schools. This morning, her unhappiness was a different one, though. As her flamboyant saree would indicate, she's not of an acquiescent personality, and she would never content herself with merely observing, or enjoying, that Tanyss is beautiful, as many of her classmates do. She would need to explore the matter further, propelled by her intelligent, inevitable extrapolation right into the context of her fate's ironic joke.

"I'm not beautiful," she said hotly. "I'm ugly, with my black skin."

Several women, less beautiful, nodded in pity of her affliction. She is darker than most of her classmates.

When she began at our slum school, Amena was, like most of the other mothers, completely illiterate, but, unlike most others, she evinced subtle signs of embarrassment at her limitations, would seem to smart at getting something wrong. In this way, her persistence seemed particularly praiseworthy, but it also shows that she measured herself by an external standard.

"Everyone knows you're beautiful, Amena," I said. "You and your black skin are beautiful."

"No one needs to tell me I'm beautiful, because I know I'm ugly," she said, and she pinched angrily at the skin on her bare forearm.

I said, "Dear Amena, right now wealthy European women are paying large sums of money to get their pale skin colour closer to yours."

"I'll trade you right now," she said. "My black skin for your white skin."

The other women laughed. Amena smiled at the success of her humour, but her eyes flashed.

"I won't make that trade, because I would lose on it," I said.

"Yes, you see!" she said in bitter triumph.

"I would lose because, as it is, everyday I get to look at Amena in her beautiful black skin, and she only gets to look at me. I'm already getting the better of the deal."

This delighted all the women. Even Amena joined their pealing laughter.

Of course, Amena could look in the scrap of broken mirror tied with jute to a bamboo pole in her little hovel and recognize with her own eyes that she is beautiful, which is why she was so angry with the framework, that value placed on light skin as a feature of beauty in and of itself, that said she wasn't, angry that her beauty, unlike Tanyss' beauty in Tanyss' world, doesn't count for a fig in hers.

Amena is, to look at her, a young woman. Most women of her age in her situation are about three-quarters through their lives, however. Unseen inside them, the effects of poverty and ignorance are ticking off their days at double time.

One afternoon not long after, Tanyss and I were walking along the main road of the neighbourhood, and several of our mother students, including Amena, who were begging outside the exclusive market, saw us coming and ran to greet us, as is their sweet habit. We were standing on the footpath, surrounded, idly talking about this or that, when, out on the road, a woman in a passing rickshaw urgently signalled the wallah to pull over to where we stood. She was a Bangladeshi woman, or possibly Indian, expensively dressed, and she carried a parasol against the sun, probably to preserve the dubious effect of skin-lightening cream.

"Don't give these women any money!" she commanded Tanyss and me (in English, the enclave of the elite) when she drew up to us. "They are not poor!"

In our surprised silence, she continued, "They're professional beggars. I see them daily outside the supermarket."

She looked at them contemptuously.

"They are not poor!" she said again.

I didn't say, in response, what I felt disposed to say. I limited myself to "Thank you for your concern for us, but these women are all students at our schools."

"Oh!" she said, clearly startled and confused.

Tanyss stepped over to speak to the woman. I knew what she was doing, besides exercising a patience I don't have: we know that the most beneficial social element for the poor is an enlightened middle class. Bangladesh is in the process of emerging awkwardly, painfully, from a feudal society, like something indeterminate hatched from an egg ---- what is that?

some reptile? some bird? ---- with a small middle class that is growing slowly, but isn't enlightened. So, in fact, the woman is important in her little way, alas. Tanyss has the fortitude to try, in her reasonable tones, to convince one caste-conscious bigot at a time.

For my part, I might have enjoyed ---- but possibly not ---- asking the woman if she knew where and how those women lived, why, if they weren't poor, they'd subject themselves daily to sneering scorn from the likes of her and the batons of the guards and harassment from the police in the hope of getting a couple of cents from passing living-allowance misers who'd just paid ten dollars for a tiny tub of mundane Australian margarine rather than endure the odd taste of the inexpensive local butter; why it was important to her that we be prevented from giving them anything, whatever their circumstance; and if it was to rationalize her own parsimony that she propagated the misshapen myth weed that the poor aren't poor.

Instead, I just turned my attention back to our students. Where some of the women merely seemed subdued, Amena, glistening black in the beating sun, glared at the plump, protected, artificially-pallid woman in the rickshaw; Munni may well have laid into her, in English to show, shockingly, her breach in the citadel of privilege, but Amena, much less combative, glared, breathing hard. I interposed myself and said "Come, dear, don't fuss about someone like that." She smiled up at me with angry eyes.

"Just picture her arguing her rickshaw wallah down from twenty taka to ten, and consider how important she is," I suggested.

Amena is genuinely poor, genuinely dark, genuinely beautiful, and she finds herself having the odd luxury of genuinely presenting her life to people who care to do something with it. Perhaps that is the further extrapolation of the ironic joke that amuses her so, that, ultimately, the joke's really on the woman in the rickshaw, about whom nothing, be it her values, ideas, ostensible concern, or fair-skinned aristocracy, is genuine at all.

In our schools, there are cheap, low plastic stools reserved for Tanyss' and my use, whenever we are there; everyone else sits on the bamboo mats. The stools aren't there by our provision; they grew like toadstools of inescapable courtesy, as far as I know.

It became the habit of the mothers, if their babes in arms were restive for reasons other than hunger, to pass the fretful bundles forward to me, so they could continue their schoolwork. They seemed to find a humorous incongruity in the picture of a white man in a suit holding a brown baby on his lap, but the trick usually worked, and the babies would settle into silent observation, often gumming my finger. These people can't afford diapers, of course, and the first time the inevitable occurred on my trouser leg, the mother of the leaking baby stared in apprehension, awaiting my reaction. When I showed no concern, the women all had a good giggle, and thereafter I think they actually looked forward to the event as a sure-fire comical interlude.

At less than two dollars to get a suit dry-cleaned, I had no reason to be disturbed. At least the expression of urine is a sign of a properly-functioning system; much more distressing were the other emissions from the babies and toddlers, the pus from the ears, the discharge from the eyes, the bloody abscesses in the little mouths. To advise the mothers against bathing themselves and their children in the foul bodies of water available to them would be as practical as telling them not to breathe the

187

corrupted air, not to crouch over their clay ovens smouldering scrap Styrofoam as fuel, not to drink the arsenic-laced well water; healthy choices are luxuries unavailable to these people.

Toddlers accompanying their mothers got into the habit, too, of draping themselves on Tanyss' or my knees, affection leaning in for affection. When we sit on our low stools, our laps are the ideal height for little ones to stand and rest their dear heads. That we have a soft spot for children ---- well, actually, it's a soft spot for most people, but is fully demonstrable with children ---- became well known, and wasn't lost on Rashida.

Rashida was the manageress of one section of the slum in which our first school was opened. It seems absurd to think that there is a commercial structure to the collection of illegal shanty squats, but each of those leaning, leaking contrivances of bamboo and rusty corrugated tin has an absentee owner with no legitimate claim to the land on which they're built, and a resident manager who duns the monthly rents and generally holds sway through his or her absolute authority of eviction.

Rashida's hegemony was compounded by the fact that her brother was a low-level official of the thoroughly corrupted city police. She was distinguished, too, by being quite stout in a slum of rake-thin women, and by knowing some English even before our school opened; on that basis, she, laughing, would decline my invitations to attend our school, even when I'd tell her that there was more than English instruction going on and warned her that the English of the attending women would surpass hers one day.

Rashida's brother would appear in the doorway of the school from time to time, and I made a point of greeting him warmly each time he did, while indicating that he wasn't welcome to enter. (Except for those associated with Amarok Society, men aren't allowed in our schools.) With each visit, he would stress meaningfully, ominously, that we need not worry, he granted his approval, and every time he did, I would thank him with a tone of sincerity and confidence, as though I had no idea whatever else he might mean. I sensed that he couldn't quite satisfy himself about us; we're set up where international aid agencies don't go, and whereas most aid workers elsewhere dress in a manner Bangladeshis regard, with puzzlement, as slovenly, the Munros are always dressed in the manner of important people, and we always deported ourselves as such, because of our foolish belief that what we do is important. I think, too, he was intimidated by a roomful of thirty to forty emboldened women turning to assess him with open hostility; I know it would have given me pause.... At any rate, each time, he eventually wandered away empty-handed.

Rashida wielded her clout, and protected it jealously. She appreciated humility in her tenants, and Munni, who never takes a backward step, and Amena, whose defiance is like an aerobic regimen, were anathema to her. That they gained additional prominence through our school became more than she could bear, and she began often to pull me into her room as I passed in the mornings, to accuse both Munni and Amena of prostitution. She plainly expected me to send the two from our school in disgrace, and was plainly confused when I didn't, so she increased the severity of the accusations and provided opportunities for verification.

It wasn't that I necessarily disbelieved her. I wasn't sure that the accusations weren't true; but, as Gabriel said, "Rashida doesn't know that she might as well be saying 'Those two women need your school even more than you thought.'" I was concerned by the accusations, however, as the treatment of unprotected prostitutes is so harsh. Were Rashida to place her angry assertions before her brother, her antipathy could have turned disastrous. So I never ceased to smile, never ceased to invite her to join our school.

Everyone in Bangladesh, no matter how uneducated, knows that during the war for independence, the Pakistani army killed three million Bangladeshis, the worst genocide in history. Some BD historians can't accept the number as possible, and even at that number it doesn't rank as the worst genocide, but, still, those who know very little else know that, and that they hate Pakistanis.

Through her work, Tanyss came to know and befriend a bright and pleasant Pakistani man, Haider, who was posted to Dhaka with a major charity organization, along with his beautiful and gracious Kashmiri wife, Kausar. That he was of the detested nationality was of little effect to Haider, as in his duties he interacted entirely with other internationals, and their residence was in the heavily-guarded international area; but Kausar was effected, as she was a trained and skilful medical doctor who was prevented from practicing in doctor-deprived Dhaka, and only, she felt, because she was native to that disputed region of Pakistan. One social evening, Kausar expressed to us again, in her refined way, her frustration with her enforced inactivity.

Tanyss said: "You know, the women and children at our slum schools suffer constant illness. Would you consider visiting them for medical consultations on a voluntary basis?"

And Kausar, bless her heart, said that she would.

We arranged for her to visit the first school the next week.

190

Our mothers were abuzz with anticipation on the scheduled morning. Our day-to-day teacher at the school was a sharp young man named Rony, and I dispatched him to await Kausar and Tanyss at the edge of the slum, to escort them safely into our school. They were being accompanied by our administrator, Ruma, who would provide precise translation, as Kausar spoke English and Urdu, the language with which Pakistan had failed to eliminate Bangla forty years earlier.

Kausar is from a privileged background, and slums such as Dhaka's are outside her experience. Few outside people visit our schools, but when they do, their first reactions to the slums are mostly similar: shock and fear. When Kausar arrived at our school, she was unable to conceal that she was much disturbed, but she conducted herself courageously, nonetheless. Tanyss provided a nice introduction for our press of sitting students and their babies; and then, into the ensuing uncertain silence, I said "Rony, now would be a fine time for you and me to take a long walk.", which elicited relieved laughter throughout.

When we returned ninety minutes later, Kausar was just stepping out of our little classroom oven. She was both very shaken and deeply moved.

"Those people have serious health problems," she said to me, as though it were a surprise to her despite all we'd told her.

She gave me an extensive rundown of diagnoses and treatments. She was able to provide some medicines herself, but others we would have to obtain by hook or by crook. Bangladesh has no such regulation as prescriptions.

Then she said: "O, they're so sweet."

Indeed. I stepped into the school. It was obvious the love was entirely reciprocated. Our mothers' faces glowed with hope and gratitude.

I asked them: "Do you know that your benefactress is Pakistani?"

They were utterly taken aback, disbelief on their faces.

"It almost makes you wonder whom to hate," Tanyss said.

People at our level clean their teeth with ashes. Every morning, as I went to one of our little schools, I would pass people with blackened fingers reaching into blackened mouths, rubbing and rubbing. From the looks on their faces ---- not from any personal experience, for sure ---- I assumed the process was an unpleasant one, and whatever chemical residues might be contained in the ashes, fluoride isn't likely to be one of them.

I was talking about this unhappy necessity with Maksuda, our very first teacher, as we walked from the school at which she taught. As if conjured by our conversation, we right away came upon a peddler with a pushcart heaped with cheap toothbrushes, something neither of us had ever seen before. Maksuda closed her eyes for a moment and gave a tiny shake of her head, but made no comment; like others, she has seen enough of the apparent coincidences of Amarok Society to believe that our every step is by some design, or designer. We took it as our cue, anyway, and I drove a hard bargain, something one can do with a peddler who has started his day without any real expectation of selling a few hundred toothbrushes to one white foreigner first thing.

The day we handed out the toothbrushes at Munni's school, Rony and I might have been Santa Clauses ---- I hesitate to suggest Tooth Fairy ---- for the

192

pleasure we created. Munni's sister, Roxanna, who is my daughter and was also, briefly, my intended second wife (but that's another story) every evening conducted a homework session at the school, at which most mothers dutifully attended; as it was much cheaper for us to buy one big tube of toothpaste than many small ones, Roxanna applied dabs for our mothers' and their children's toothbrushes at the end of the evening session. So when Kausar provided us with calcium pills and vitamins, Roxanna just added them to the distribution.

Something we like to see is the rapid-developing sense of entitlement in our students. For instance, when a woman joins our class, she is presented with a notebook, a pencil, a pencil sharpener and an eraser, and she normally receives these as gifts; when it comes time to replace them, however, she'll normally receive them as the fulfilment of her right. It seems a small thing, but heightened expectations for one's life have a direct correlation to increased willingness to work to achieve them (spoiled brats aside).

One morning, at the end of a lesson, Rashida appeared in the classroom. She carried a terribly thin, tiny baby.

"You hold," she said, smiling, holding the little one out to me.

It was a baby girl, and she was nothing in the crook of my arm. She was dressed in a torn, filthy frilly dress that had been meant for a baby three times her size, before it had been used to scrub someone's rickshaw.

Women who had been about to depart gathered around in observation.

"Who is she?" I asked.

"Reena," Rashida said.

193

"Who is her mother?"

Rashida shook her head dismissively, and then, smiling again, said "You take."

"I take?"

"You, Madame, take," she said, nodding.

The tiny one looked up at me with little black eyes.

Nearly two decades before and in a school half a world away, a message was relayed to me by one of her teaching staff that Tanyss wished me to come to her office. When I came through her office door, I saw that she was sitting in a chair with her back to me, looking down, and sitting facing her were some elders of the isolated arctic community. I stepped behind her and looked over her shoulder, and saw little black eyes looking up at me.

And in that instant, I was a father. I now look slightly upward into those same beautiful eyes; never from that moment to this did I once doubt that I was looking at my own son.

Rashida nodded with pleasure, as though the matter were settled.

The matter wasn't settled. Although anyone's heart would have gone out immediately to the poor little soul, I couldn't feel as I had those years before; some unbidden recognition was missing.

"Who is her mother?" I asked again.

"Madame be mother," Rashida said cheerfully.

I looked at my students gathered round. In the arctic community, I had seen a sense of something momentous in the faces of the elders, a sort of serious miracle. The expressions of the women around me were watchful, guarded and resigned. Amena observed me sharply.

194

"Apa, take Reena," I said to Rashida, and she reluctantly did.

"You bring Madame here?"

"Yes, I shall. I'll bring her tomorrow."

That evening, I told Tanyss what had transpired.

For an accomplished career woman, Tanyss has the most excitable and responsive maternal instinct. If circumstances had permitted, I know I'd right now be combing the final pages of a frayed baby name book for the last available. ("Zechariah? No, I'm pretty sure we've got one already....") So it was natural for her to at least explore the possibilities with an open mind. I told her I would defer not to her instinct, but to her intuition.

The next morning, we went to the class, and, sure enough, Rashida awaited us there with tiny Reena.

She straight away placed Reena in Tanyss' arms, and stroked Tanyss' shoulder reassuringly.

"Madame mummy," she said with what might have been intended as a warm-hearted laugh.

Some babies don't cry because there's no need, and some other babies, alas, don't cry because there's no point. Reena did with Tanyss as she'd done with me, merely looked upward, and sucked at nothing with her tiny mouth a bit, preparing for a lifetime of working on whatever scraps came its way. I tried to get her to grip my finger in her hand, but she made no attempt.

"Mummy Madame love babu," Rashida purred.

"Yes, I love her, of course," Tanyss said, but, in her heart, intuition indeed triumphed over instinct. "But who else loves her?"

Rashida shook her head, smiling still.

"I want to see this babu's mother."

"No, no," Rashida said. "No mother."

I looked over to Amena, who watched as she had the day before.

"Who is her mother?" I asked her.

Amena cast a dark look at Rashida, and answered "Kurshida."

Rashida's smile disappeared.

"I want to see Kurshida," Tanyss insisted.

"Father, I take you," Munni volunteered, and Rashida glowered.

Munni led us along narrow bamboo walkways to a nearby room. Rashida hustled in ahead of us. There was a young man sitting on a little cot, and on the plank floor crouched a skinny, angular young woman, unfamiliar to me, who barely glanced at us as we entered, showed no recognition of Reena before setting her eyes down at the floor. She held herself strangely.

"Kurshida," Tanyss asked in Bangla, "is Reena your babu?"

Kurshida didn't respond at all.

Rashida touched her own forehead with her fingers and shook her head emphatically.

"Kurshida stupid," she said. She bent over and lifted Kurshida's bony left arm. Her hand was frozen in a sort of open clutch. "See, arm no good." She pointed to Kurshida's chest. "No milk left breast. Right breast not enough, Reena hungry."

Kurshida endured this inventory without demur.

"Kurshida, do you want to give Reena to us?" Tanyss asked.

"She not want Reena," Rashida insisted.

Tanyss said to me "What do you make of this?"

I said "Why is everyone but Rashida looking so unhappy?"

I looked at the glum faces of Munni, Amena and the other mothers who'd followed us and pressed inside the doorway.

196

"These women love you, and they surely love Reena, so why aren't they happy?"

"What of Kurshida?" Tanyss asked.

"Obviously, she's non compos mentis, but the question is why."

Tanyss crouched down before her, took Kurshida's right hand in her free hand, and searched her face for a long minute.

"She's heart-broken," Tanyss said, her eyes welling. "She's grief-stricken."

She settled Reena into the crook of Kurshida's right arm, and only then did Kurshida react, looking down at her babu.

"Keep your Reena, Kurshida," she said.

"Madame," Rashida said sternly, "Reena die."

"Not if we provide her with milk formula," Tanyss said. "Tell Kurshida that we will bring her baby formula and bottled water, but in exchange, she must attend our school."

Rashida shook her head.

"No school. Kurshida stupid."

Tanyss said, "Munni, please tell Kurshida."

Munni did so, and Kurshida smiled faintly and nodded.

"That doesn't seem so stupid," Tanyss said.

We left amid Rashida's continuing objections. Munni along walked with us, as was her habit.

"Father," she confided, "Rashida say she charge you one lakh taka, Reena."

"Is that so?"

"Rashida talk big."

"Quite," I said.

"And Kurshida could do nothing about it?" asked Tanyss.

"We very poor, apa," she said simply, "very, very poor."

"So poor you have to sell your babies, daughter?" I asked. "How can that be, when you beg daily outside the market?"

We took Munni with us to the exclusive market, so she could deliver the water and formula back to Kurshida. We stopped at the footpath before it.

"Do you want to come in with me?" I asked her.

She looked at its uniformed guards, the expensive chauffeured SUVs circling in its driveway.

She shook her head, her mouth tight. "No, Father."

"All right, dear, not today, but one day...."

It turned out that Kurshida had been left crippled by a childhood bout of typhoid fever. If there was also intellectual impairment, it wasn't severe, and she became one of the keenest and happiest of our students, handing forward her notebook for my approval amongst the first or second wave after an assigned exercise. Her good right hand was capable of neat printing, and she quickly progressed from drawing her letters to printing them. As I recall, it was Kurshida who finally gave voice to the popular sentiment that my check marks weren't fully valid, in that they weren't in red. Ruma got in a supply of red pens, and the mothers in all our schools were satisfied.

We insisted that Kurshida nurse Reena as much as she could before resorting to the bottle each time, and we believed she was conscientious in that. Soon enough, forlorn Kurshida and starving Reena were pretty much just another mother and baby in the class.

Trouble, however, was brewing.

A few weeks later, Rashida came to know that Munni had alerted us to the plan to endear Reena to us, and then extort from us the one lakh taka (about $2000) to keep her. I would bet it had come from Munni herself rashly rubbing Rashida's nose in it. Rashida's furious response was to evict Munni and her three children and Roxanna from their hovel, on the spot.

Our short-term solution was to have the homeless family move into our school, which was beyond the section of slum under Rashida's management. This further maddened Rashida, who then declared that anyone of her section who attended our school would be evicted.

Several of our students stayed away, including Amena and Kurshida.

We decided that the key absentee was Amena, that if she, of the natural defiance, was intimidated, we'd not embolden the others against Rashida's tyranny.

Tanyss collected Munni and together they went to see Amena at her room.

"If you tell the other women you're going back to school, they will come, too," Tanyss said to her.

"If I go back to school, I'll have no house," Amena said.

"You'll all keep your houses, if you all act together. Rashida won't want to tell the landlord that suddenly half the houses aren't paying him any money, believe me."

Feisty Munni spoke vehemently in Bangla, spat the name Rashida, until Amena's gleaming smile grew across her face.

Rashida stood shooting daggers from her doorway as Tanyss, Munni and Amena went along to each of our students in turn.

The next morning, all were back at school. Gabriel and I took the class from Rony, in case of further trouble.

It arrived in the form of Rashida's brother, the police official, stepping inside the school, where he didn't belong, to stand in stern disapproval. I continued the lesson for a minute or two, but Gabriel went back and stood right beside him as a guardian archangel. Rashida's brother took one furtive sideways peek at him, and that was just the uncertainty we wanted to see. I assigned a little task to our students and stepped through them to our scowling trespasser.

"I'm pleased to see you," I said. "I was thinking of you the other day as the Minister and I were discussing our school here."

He faltered.

"The Minister?"

"Yes," I said. "I thought I should send a note down to your superiors."

"A note?"

"Telling them of our appreciation for your cooperation and support. It might help you."

"Help?"

"Yes," I stressed meaningfully, ominously. "You need not worry. You have our approval."

"Yes," said Gabriel, closing the last centimetre between them.

"Just wait outside until the end of the lesson," I instructed, "and you can give me your superiors' contact information."

He slipped away some time when I was no longer paying attention to him.

"The Minister?" Gabriel asked after the lesson.

"Now, my son, I've raised you never to lie, and I'm no hypocrite. Your mother and I met a Bangladeshi Baptist minister last week. And I'm quite sure I must have mentioned something about our schools."

"O, Dad," he said sadly, "by that means you pursued only the litter of the law ... which, I guess, was the idea, really ...."

200

I mightn't have bothered, but my patient and forbearing Tanyss went to visit Rashida. This is what she said to her:

"Sister, we know that you sit above the other women here, and that you don't deign to sit down at their level in our school. But you live in the same place they do, in the same conditions; you breathe the same air, drink the same water, bathe in the same lake, and you know that some day you'll be sick again, just as they'll be. And when you're sick, do you want to be as they are, inside our care and protection, or alone outside it?"

Nearly two decades later and a half a world away, my son Azien's beautiful black eyes absorb sights no one else from his arctic hometown has ever seen. He's a most talented photographer. He's no dispassionate eye. Somehow his camera captures not just the image before it but also the sensitivity and compassion behind it. One day, he came home very upset after photographing a little boy so hungry, he was eating Styrofoam packing worms he'd found. Azien keeps a pocketful of ten taka notes to pay his subjects after the fact is caught. The little boy would be able to afford rice with ten taka, but I suppose he would have to wait until he no longer had a bellyful of Styrofoam for rice to do him any good. I don't know how long it would take for packing worms to pass through his system; I don't know of any scientific studies of such a diet that could tell us for sure.

Our bodies are designed to thrive on good nutrition. Our minds are designed to thrive on good nutrition of meaningful information and knowledge; when starved of it, they will desperately resort to Styrofoam packing worms. Ignorance is bliss as much as chronic malnutrition is.

With something nutritious to chew on for a change, wicked Rashida's mind began to function, if not immediately to thrive; it had, after all, many foam worms to move aside, and we couldn't expect her to figure out any time soon, for instance, that it's not as bad to sell one's body as it is to sell someone else's. She's a bright woman, though, if not a wholesome one, and she soon saw where her advantage truly lay.

She raised her hand to pat Tanyss' arm.

"Madame, we are sisters."

Amena is, to look at her, a young woman. Most women of her age in her situation are three-quarters through their lives. Unseen inside them, the effects of poverty and ignorance are ticking off their days at double time. Perhaps our school and our programmes have already given her a new lease on life. We give her body something with which to work, and her sharp mind something with which to work, and we provide both with defences against the constant threats, and she should be longer-lived for them. Her children will have the benefit of her and her progress for a longer time, and so the effect will perpetuate itself. But woman does not live by bread and book alone. Every year our schools celebrate the anniversary of their opening with a gala party for which our students make exceptional and creative effort, set Roxanna to overheat the AS sewing machine, to dress their very best. They receive awards and prizes for their achievements, and they perform recitations, songs and dances. It's an occasion for a woman like Amena to know, without qualification, she's beautiful, and that being beautiful, one way or another, in her world counts for a more than a fig. That should give her an extra decade.

Bread, book and being beautiful, one way or another: by those things woman lives. Man lives by bread, book and watching woman being beautiful. Lucky man, already getting the better of the deal.

...A VERY SAD STATE...

Mahogany Pods Roasting on an Open Fire

The people here are proud to say that their country boasts six seasons, while much of the rest of the world must struggle along with a mere four. I'm not sure what the six seasons are. It seems to me the range of their weather and temperature could all occur unremarkably in the progression of one Canadian prairie June; of course, it may be a matter of me being unable to appreciate the subtleties, much as with whatever else beyond chilli I'm supposed to be discerning when our housecleaner, Beauty, happens to cook for us.

I have noticed that at a certain time of the year, the monsoon stops and the weather becomes very dry and hot, and then, several weeks later, leaves and seed pods begin to fall from the mahogany trees that line our street, and that the armed security guards grouped at every gate are found to be wearing military-style parkas and woollen gloves, and that the rickshaw wallahs wrap their heads in such mufflers as they can obtain, and headlines in the newspapers tally the rash of deaths attributed to the "bitter cold". This is the cue to the Canadian living here that he might possibly don a light sweater without sweltering.

One morning during this time of year, our housekeeper, Ratan, reported to us that there had been frost in his village. Our questions soon revealed that what he thought of as frost was just condensation on the grass, but such was his excitement, and happiness with his new bond with his Canadian employers, we didn't disabuse him.

Not all trees here lose their leaves, and some lose them only in patches of dirty old leaves to be immediately replaced with bright new ones. However, the young mahogany trees on our street will lose their leaves and stand bare for a few weeks. If we are quick about it, we can walk through the leaves, and, stiff and hard as they might be, they can approximate the sound of a Canadian autumn stroll well enough to bring a homesick tear to the eye.

The people here seem to find the fallen leaves and woody seed pods detestable; the same guards and custodians who will patiently abide the dead dog by the footpath until the rats and crows have carried it away by the bellyful are somehow compelled to sweep together any leaves and pods, and set fire to them on a daily basis, thereby both depriving this land-of-clay of convenient compost and contributing to the already appallingly polluted atmosphere with slow smoulder enough to bring another homesick tear to the eye, but in a different way.

To my coarsened Canadian sensibility, there are two seasons in this city:

1. sog
2. smog

One day deep in the heart of smog season, or maybe deep in the black lung of it, a young family rolled under the trees across from our flat, rolled with no more apparent purpose than the pods, no obvious function beyond gravity. A young woman with her two tiny children, they settled onto the footpath opposite us, and there they remained, perhaps by fate; but if it was their fate or ours, I don't know.

The woman set up a little open nest, spreading their few possessions around them: a couple of thin blankets, a few mesh bags of plastic bowls and recovered water bottles. She wore the cheap thin cotton saree of the poor, and her babus wore cotton shorts, sometimes also little sweatshirts, and other times nothing at all. The children were girls; one was perhaps a bit older than two

206

years, the other no more than one. They were all thin and very pretty; also, as became terribly apparent, the young mother was utterly insane.

On their second night there, Tanyss and I, on our way home from teaching our evening class, came upon their little nest. They were settled down, lying together beneath a streetlamp, perhaps as a discouragement to rats, and, as a discouragement to the disease-bearing mosquitoes, were draped head to foot by one of the thin blankets. The other blanket, presumably, was beneath them. None of them stirred as we stood in unhappy inspection of the trio's situation.

The elderly guard at the office building next door to our apartment building, who seemed to work twenty-four hours a day (so a bit more than Tanyss and I), and with whom we'd struck up a friendly acquaintance, paused in his efforts to prod his seasonal smudge pile to more detrimental effect to join us in the swirling yellow light, his bearing solemn and dignified, as always. He wore a heavy, saggy sweater and scarf.

"A very sad state, very sad," he said, shaking his head. "They are very poor. She has no husband."

To be the widow of a poor man is to be in a dire circumstance, indeed, so much so that --- it is said --- it isn't uncommon for a woman to take the drastic step of not being one, of not being, instead. We knew of an instance where a widow with young children, assessing the reality of her financial outlook, decided to lose half of it, and advertised one of her eyes for sale. To be an unwed mother is to have even bleaker prospects, if anyone can.

Beside their huddled little mound was a bowl. I didn't think it was there for the purpose of begging, and later evidence suggested I was right, but I said to our companion, "If I put some money in their bowl, is there any chance it will still be there when they awake?"

"O, yes," he said. "I will watch out. Don't be concerned."

I put twenty taka in the bowl; that's about thirty-five cents, a sum not so paltry-seeming in Dhaka as it would be in Vancouver; we normally don't give alms on the street, as our own charitable projects have a nasty way of keeping us broke all the time, with one unforeseen emergency after another; our budget has come to include the classification "anticipated unanticipated", but even that never goes as planned unplanned.

It's my habit to go out on our balcony in the early morning to drink a cup of tea. The early mornings are the best time of day in smog season, as the air is slightly less dirty, the sunlight is less orange, and the birds are not yet blasted by the city's incredible cacophony-to-come; in their songs and calls, exotic, the liar birds promise a lovely day that will yet yield to its perverted imitation.

So on the morning after we made our tiny donation to the little family on the footpath, I was on the balcony, in a position to observe them as they roused themselves. The woman took the money from the bowl as though she'd expected it to be there, and then she set about to wash herself with water from her collection of bottles, and then she thoroughly washed her naked babus, who shivered in the chill. The little ones' hair was close-cropped, but her own mane was long and luxuriant, and she spent a long time brushing it. She would shortly conceal it under cotton in the obligatory convention of modesty, but clearly she had neither real modesty about her hair nor reason for any.

When the little girls were dressed, the mother beckoned to a rickshaw wallah just starting his slow prowl of the streets. He cycled over to her with an air of reserved scepticism, but she confidently swung her older girl up into the little seat, and leapt up herself with the younger one draped over her arm. She settled herself in a pose befitting Elizabeth R in that elaborate golden royal carriage of hers, and motioned imperially to the driver to proceed.

They returned in fewer than thirty minutes, and hopped down from the rickshaw, whereupon the mother began to argue with the wallah about the cost of the ride. Arguing costs with rickshaw wallahs is a ritual as faithfully observed as anything the Qur'an requires, and everyone does it without shame, with the apparent objective of creating grievance in both parties. That her debate was as vehement as any wasn't of note to me at the time. Finally, they seemed to arrive at a mutually-sufferable amount; she handed him one of the two ten taka notes we'd left her, and he pedalled away. And I asked myself why a woman in her circumstance would spend half her money on a rickshaw ride.

In the ensuing weeks, we encountered the family frequently, as we move about a lot and they didn't. At first, the little ones stared at us in gaping amazement, having never seen either white people or a Canadian Indian in the pale flesh before, but soon enough the older girl skipped up happily to us whenever we came, even took to hugging our legs and beaming beautifully up at us, and her friendliness became profitable, as I started giving her a ten-taka note whenever we met. Her baby sister was less mobile, but from time to time she would manage to toddle to us, too, maybe to hug the available leg, for which she would gain a two-taka note. (Here, the cynical voice says "Takas buy spurious displays of love cheaply in a situation of such want.", but, as usual, it creeps into the ear only to assert the essentially incorrect.) We became affectionate friends, and my family focussed much loving concern on the footpath family. I would have pressed the mother to join one of our schools, had she not taken up this inexplicable residency in our (relatively) upper-middle-class neighbourhood so disjunct from others of her desperate circumstance.

I was never sure if the mother noticed the exchanges of money, as she always seemed to be looking away as they took place.

And every now and then, from inside our flat, I would hear her arguing with someone. I never thought anything of it; these are uninhibited, outgoing people, and the women, in particular, enjoy their quarrels in a way we can only envy.

One time, however, the argument became particularly vituperative and long-lasting, with no pleasure at all in her raised voice. I left my toil to step out onto the balcony, to see whom and what had occasioned such shrill denunciation.

The mother stood on the footpath, her baby on her right hip, and she gestured emphatically with her free left hand at the object of her displeasure, who seemed, from the gestures and the focus of her glare, to be positioned in the middle of the narrow road;

There was no one there.... at least, no one whom I could perceive.

The two-year-old girl stood back a pace, watching, unmoving. The baby looked from her mother to the spot where someone else should have been, and back again, and then back again, silent and solemn.

The guard at the building next door left his post to come closer to the conflict; he watched the mother only, dismayed. Guards from other gates and others approached to form a wide half-circle, outside the mother's range. The baby, I sensed, was aware of being at the centre of their attention.

Her mother's tirade went on and on; at one point, she seemed to have concluded, and spun away from her unseen adversary, to my relief; but then either the adversary made some intolerable rejoinder, or the mother came up with another argument, for she wheeled back again and started in anew.

Maybe maids of Orleans, when called upon to do battle, crop their hair and cinch their forms into men's tunics and armour to conceal their femininity. When a woman here enters the fray, she obviously knows well that every aspect of her sexuality is a weapon in her arsenal, she flagrantly flaunts it, even against another woman. This mother had pulled her cotton shawl from her hair, so that her long black hair swung from side to side as she wagged her head in derision, she splayed out her feet as she strode, swayed her hips with such extravagance her baby must have been motion sick, pivoted her straightened shoulders to emphasize the thrust of her breast. She pushed out her lips, her face was aglow with arousal, her eyes were flashing flame.

Maybe she isn't insane. This may have held an element of ecstasy. It may have been an angel she confronted --- we have accepted that explanation in the past ---, an angel whose instructions to her were too onerous or odious to bear; maybe she had once bowed obediently and meekly, had fulfilled them without gaining the reward she'd been led to expect; maybe she'd had enough of keeping all these things in her heart, swung her baby forward to demand, "Here she is, as you commanded! When is the handmaiden relieved of her travail and indignity and hunger?"

Maybe he said, "Sorry, but we ordered a boy...."

On she went, and on, recrimination flying from her sneering mouth. I wondered how she could carry on for so long so loud without going hoarse.

211

And then it happened that the baby looked up to me, directly up, as if drawn, to where I stood observing from the balcony. Then she looked up to her mother's face, to catch her eye, and she raised her tiny hand to point to me, in the way a baby points, with the direction varying, the forefinger curled.

Look, Mummy, there's someone we don't hate. There's our friend.

Her mummy was preoccupied. However, the imprecise aim of her tiny hand was unerring toward me, and she pierced my heart cleanly; her attempt to pull her mother and herself into the sphere of the positive, the reliable and healthy, moved me almost beyond my ability to bear, beyond my ability to describe.

I forced myself to smile at her, and sent her a little wave of my hand. She smiled at me, and waved the baby's opening-and-closing-hand wave. We kept smiling and waving forever, until finally, finally, her mother ran out of the steamy vapours of her deep, dark pit of venom and sat down in a deflated slouch in the family nest, her daughters seating themselves on either side of her.

Those fascinated or entertained by the spectacle straggled away.

Now, it came to pass in those days that Christmas was approaching. There was no climactic evidence of this, of course, but I calculated it by the traditional method of having a six-year-old.

There are two non-Muslim matters that arouse fascinated curiosity in our Bangladeshi staff and student-teachers, two forbidden unknowns that would seem to promise confusing, heady pleasures denied them: one is alcohol, and the other is Christmas. To their questions about the first, my answers are dismissive: the fabled exquisite savour of that sauterne or single malt is pretentious bunk, the cheer and fellowship a myth with a mountain of contrary evidence accruing over it; I tell them about our experiences during many years of living in isolated Canadian aboriginal communities where alcohol is the demanding and merciless tyrant, and that, if they wish to concoct a morass of misery not yet even suspected in our most unfortunate homeland, they just need to add alcohol to the floodwaters and stir. I tell them Mohammed (PBUH) knew what he was doing when it came to booze. (Here, my teenaged son Gabriel asks, all angelic innocence, "What of Jesus turning water into wine?" "Jewish wine," I reply, "a quaff so unpalatable, it has effectively prevented Jewish alcoholism throughout the ages. So Jesus knew what he was doing, too.") The usual reaction to my diatribe is ashen nods all 'round and shots of Fear-of-Allah that I know will lose their preventative potency like old vaccines; the morbid curiosity will return, and I'll give the same answer.

What of the questions about Christmas? They ask if it is like Eid. I tell them that it is unlike any other festival in the world; that no other festival so powerfully exerts its atmosphere and spirit; that no other festival has inspired such superb creative expression; that in our other homeland, Canada, Tanyss and I have Jewish and atheist friends who celebrate Christmas (that people whom they admire should make friends of both Jews and atheists at first disoriented them, but that's another story); but isn't it all about the birth of Jesus, they ask, the festival of a lesser prophet mistakenly credited with divinity by the flawed faithful?

I tell them that the best known verse in the world is "'Twas the night before Christmas,/ and all through the house....", from a Christmas poem that never mentions Jesus; that one of the most beloved stories and books --- so intrinsic now that I must teach them the main character's name as a necessary part of an English vocabulary --- is all about Christmas spirits, and refers to Jesus once or twice only in passing; that the best-selling recording in the world for many years --- until The Beatles displaced it --- was a Christmas song that never mentions Jesus and was written by a Jew.

Is it just about feasting and shopping, then?

If it's just about feasting and shopping, then Eid has it matched, at least for the small proportion of the population that can afford the model Eid. I point out that Eid shopping is for oneself. Most people in North America have the means for a bit of shopping and feasting for themselves at Christmas, but that more people end their own lives at Christmas than at any other time of the year, simply because of feeling isolated and separated from its spirit.

I observe that one Dhaka daily newspaper wrote about the "Spirit of Eid", failed in its attempt to define it, but illustrated it with a cartoon of Dr. Seuss' grinch wearing a prayer cap instead of a Santa hat. I tell them that there are no newspapers in the non-Muslim world using some amended artefact of Eid to embody the Spirit of Christmas.

Christmas in a tropical Muslim nation, real Christmas, would seem to be difficult.

Of course, considerable effort is needed to celebrate Christmas with all the trimmings even in an environment where one is inundated with them, but here one must actively, diligently seek the trimmings out, and even when they're found, the risk of disappointment is high, as with, for instance, the visit to the Sannatarium, the pirates of penance pantomime, and the frustration of the featherweight turkey:

214

The Visit to the Sannatarium: Alastair, six, was naturally worried about Santa's means of locating and getting to him, surrounded as we were by vast miles of Islam, then Hinduism, and then official atheism. In exploratory discussion with Ratan, who is one of the small number of Christian Bangladeshis and whose village is Christian, he had woefully discovered that Santa had never visited Ratan's young daughter, and the way that Ratan had smiled pityingly upon him had disconcerted.

Now, the U.S. makes a big, deep footprint wherever it goes in the world, but sometimes it's of a sooty boot. A decree went out that the American Club was hosting a children's Christmas party, with games and activities and a special visit from St. Nick himself, and that all members of any of the international clubs were welcome to bring their children. This seemed the very thing to ease our little boy's troubled mind, and we knew that it was an event quite beyond the imagination or effort of our laissez-faire (more like lazy and unfair, but that's another story) Canadian High Commission, so we packed ourselves into Wahid's rickshaw on the appointed afternoon, and off we went, pretending it was a sleigh ride but conscientiously not pretending Wahid was a horse lean and lank. Once within the fortress walls of the club, Alastair would have none of the face-painting or card-making or other crafty activities or games set up on the lawns; his only interest was in the jolly old elf himself. We found out that he was receiving visitors in air-conditioned comfort inside the clubhouse.

We found him sitting on an ordinary chair, with a little American girl on his knee. He wasn't the worst Santa I've ever seen --- the worst I've seen enacted the entire catalogue of Claus in defect including drunken, lewd wisecracks, so the present one was clearing a very low hurdle to escape that designation --- but his appearance

215

surely wouldn't have reawakened faith in the heart of any young doubter. He was suitably overweight, but his belly lacked jollity, his ho-ho-ho lacked authority, and his eye lacked that magical twinkle. His manner was friendly enough, but in a style very, well, American, rather than very kind-old-saint, less "let's feed the reindeer" than "let's grill some deerburgers on the tailgate". And his performance was far from 'method': he failed to find his inner Santa and permit him to take over his personality. Also, he referred to himself as 'Sanna', in the way of Hollywood movies. Any Canadian child knows that's not the North Polish pronunciation. Still, he offered a worried child evidence that Santa could find his way to the centre of Dhaka, after all, so I was charitable and grateful to him. I wish to stress that he had my good will from the outset.

"Where are you from?" Santa was asking the girl on his knee.

She answered that she was from some town in New England.

"No kidding!" Santa exclaimed in excited recognition. "I've been there!" He then proceeded to give a short list of other nearby towns he'd visited.

The problem with having a really bright son ---- come to think of it, it's only one of the problems ---- is that he's very quick to pick up on errors in logic. Usually those errors are mine, of course, so I've become practised in attempted rapid recovery in response to Alastair's sharp look of silent critical enquiry. When Santa stated the places he'd been, Alastair's head shot up just a millimetre, but enough for me to detect.

Santa went on acting as though it was altogether too coincidental that he's been to the girl's hometown. The girl seemed pretty happy about it, as well, finding nothing amiss, and I glanced with only the briefest, transitory moment of envy at her waiting parents.

Santa gave the girl a candy cane ---- honestly, those Americans do provide for themselves: the candy canes must have been flown in from the U.S. ---- and called for Alastair to come forward.

I could see from Alastair's reserve on Santa's knee that suspicion was already sprouting in that hothouse brain of his.

"And what's your name?"

"Alastair Munro."

"Alas--- that's, uh, that's a different sort of name...."

"It is?" asked Alastair.

"But familiar to you from all of Alastair's letters," I offered hastily.

"Huh." Then, "Where are you from, Al?"

"Vancouver."

A puzzled look, then relief. "Washington State!"

"British Columbia," Alastair said.

"Oh." Disappointment at the interruption in his homesick revel. "I've never been to Canada. But I've been to Bellingham. That's close."

"What?" said Alastair.

"And by that you mean," I suggested urgently, "you live at the North Pole, which is really close, right, Santa? And that, certainly, you visit your closest neighbour, Canada, every Christmas Eve."

Bewildered by geographical confusion coming up hard against American chauvinism, Santa looked at me dumbly. He turned back to our little boy.

"You ever been to Bellingham, Al?" he asked, apparently trying to find some stable point of reorientation.

Alastair looked to Tanyss in enquiry.

217

"Yes," she said. "Briefly."

"O, that's good," Santa said. "Bellingham's a good town."

"And by that you mean no one misses Bellingham who's got Vancouver," I said, "as you well know from your annual trips to Vancouver, right, Santa?"

He grappled with this.

"Huh," he said.

"Eh," I riposted.

Alastair is a polite little fellow, and never means to offend, but at this he contrived to unobtrusively slide off Santa's knee and stand a couple of stealthy steps away from him, with which I could find nothing to disagree.

"So, uh, what do you want for Christmas, Al?"

I braced myself for reckless, impracticable promises from this unreasoning Santa.

Alastair considered.

"Actually, I wish you could do something for all the poor children in Dhaka."

I would guess that behind Santa's unmoving beard, his mouth fell open, as his eyes widened.

"That's what you want for Christmas?"

"Yes," Alastair said.

"Did you hear that?" Santa asked Tanyss and me. He turned to some women standing nearby. "Did you hear what he said?"

"Wow," a woman said.

"Wow," said Santa. "That's something. That's a real good wish, Al. You sure get a candy cane for that."

Outside, after we took our leave, Tanyss confirmed, "That was a nice wish, darling."

"Was it?" he asked around his candy cane. He sucked a moment on the more pressing question. "Why did Santa say where he has and hasn't been...? Hasn't he been----?"

"Because he's gone crazy," I said. "He's got bats in his Bellingham, toys in the attic instead of his workshop."

"And by that you mean----," Tanyss began patiently.

"And by that I mean he's suffering from dementia induced by heat stroke," I amended. "I've seen it before: it's a temporary condition; he should recover completely if they place him in a cool room and cover his eyes with a good world atlas."

We discussed the Santa logistics further in the days to come, including the question of his means of transportation within Bangladesh. I told Alastair that he was reputed to attach kangaroos to his sleigh when in Australia.

Every year, I assign to our children the task of composing a Christmas poem to be recited on Christmas Eve. I do this as a form of childhood inoculation against the virulent and destructive adult strain of poesy.

Here's what Alastair came up with:

Christmas Poem about Santa Claustralia

When Santa's Down Under
It makes me wonder
Does he really use
A team of kangaroos?
It would be too bumpy
Because kangaroos are too jumpy.
Wouldn't the toys shake,
Fall out of the bag, and break?
Elves would have to make
Them again. I think in my head
He could use camels instead.
It would be smoother, and, I fear
Australia's too hot for reindeer.

<u>The Pirates of Penance Pantomime:</u> It had been our tradition, every year on Christmas Eve, to watch the definitive movie of Dickens' 'A Christmas Carol', starring Alastair Sim as Scrooge (and, no, it wasn't in homage that we named our son 'Alastair', although Sim's performance is notably preferable to that of, say, a Dhaka Sanna Claus). When a family arrives to live in Bangladesh with nothing but whatever can be crammed into a suitcase per person, a copy of that classic isn't likely to be included, and wasn't in the case, or six cases, of our family. However, priorities change with the indiscernible passage of the six putative seasons here, and it began to prey on my mind that our Christmas would seem terribly deprived without it. I got the bright idea, about six weeks before Christmas, to comb file-sharing sites online and download a pirated copy of the necessary item, and then burn a video disc of the download. I rationalized that it wouldn't really be theft, surely, as it must have slipped into the public domain by then, and, anyway, I'd paid for several copies of it through the years, and, anyway, my Christmas in the Poorhouse scenario seemed to justify the theft of the bread. Also, of course, my sense of propriety has been eroded in this land where copyright dies: in shop after shop, pirated DVDs of the latest movies, complete with FBI warning, can be had for a dollar and a half.

It was with a kind of stupid optimism I began to key my search into the file-sharing sites, as a sort of Alastair Simpleton, and I was thoroughly shocked --- o, was I ever so innocent --- when my search returned copious lists of titles such as "Christmas Cookin'! Hot blonde finds surprise in her --- " and others less delicately phrased. Bear in mind that in this Muslim country, lascivious material must, as with Christmas, be

220

deliberately sought out, and doesn't spring up at one's window unbidden, so I was abnormally sensitive to the ideas the titles and descriptions prompted in my incorrigible imagination. I might have quit the exercise there, except that interspersed throughout the pornography were some wholesome items, odd things of no value to us, like Mister Magoo's Christmas Carol dubbed into Latvian; also, I found that different searches of the same title in the same file-sharing sites scared up different lists; so the results were just encouraging enough --- no, that's wrong --- were just not quite discouraging enough to cause me to give up.

The process of my dissolution was imperceptible at first, of course. Tantalized by remotely associated titles turning up, such as "Der Muppetenkerstmassleider", I began to indulge daydreams of my poor family gathered (for no good reason except the convenience of my reverie) around our blank television screen, attempting but failing to conceal their aching sighs through the wasteland Christmas Eve has become, when I slyly say, "Grace, sweetheart, why don't you just press play on the DVD player?" "But why, dear Father?" "Because it's Christmas, sweetheart." Gasps of incredulity as the familiar, portentous "buh-puh-bum-puh-bum-pub-puh-bum" Addinsell score pounds out, as the anonymous left hand reaches for the leather-bound volume on the shelf, cries of joy in the sudden awareness, gazes of worshipping wonder upon the paterfamilias who has somehow wrought this marvel....

The absolute necessity of my success began to mushroom in my mind.

I searched for days and days, started to stay up later and later at night, to get up earlier and earlier in the morning, double-clicking "Repeat Search" like an assembly-line automaton, except glassier-eyed. And then it happened, one of those curses that masquerade at first as the best fortune: reduced through the days to fuzzy, numb speculation on whether a surprise copy of the readily-available "Christmas Stalking IV: Melchior's Revenge" might possibly evoke a similar seasonal spirit in my loved ones, I peered blearily at the latest list, and there, tucked away in the bottom third of it, like a little diamond in the rough, was the entry "Scrooge 1951". My heart leapt, my hand leapt for the mouse, and I clicked the entry like a nerd-on-fire.

The site set forth the information that the download had begun. I chortled, in a sobbing sort of way.

Technology in Dhaka is not state-of-the-art; it's more like state-of-the-ark. Its internet technology, I have always suspected, was purchased second-hand from Soviet Surplus sometime before the fall of The Wall. Its highest-speed service might well be outstripped by a hand-cranked modem crafted from an old meccano set. When my download began, the file-sharer posted the rate and the estimated time to completion: the rate was .3 kilobytes per second, and the time to completion was 362 days, or just in time for the next year's Christmas, if all went well and there were no power blackouts. Of course, there are blackouts every day, for hours. As I was roughly estimating how many days I had remaining in my life-expectancy, taking into account the deleterious effects of my downloading experience to date, the screen flickered and the download message changed to "Waiting On Busy Hosts". "Waiting for busy hosts," I corrected, ever the English teacher. "Hosts wait on you." Those hosts weren't waiting on me, though. The download rate registered as zero, the percentage completed, zero. "What do you mean, bumping me aside?" I cried indignantly. "I was here first! Or there first! Or whatever!"

Shouting at somebody's computer on the other side of the world, if indeed that was what I was doing --- I'm still not perfectly clear as to how all this works --- should be heeded as a warning sign, I say in regretful hindsight. It seemed effective at the time, however, as the message of reconnection appeared, and at the blinding speed of a full kilobyte per second, reducing the etc (estimated time of completion) to a mere hundred days, and I amended my daydream to the desert of Easter, and "Why don't you press play….", glad cries as everyone ignores the inappropriateness, etc (et cetera). Such was my desperation and fatigue. Then it shifted to "Waiting on Busy Hosts" again, then, horribly, to "Need More Sources".

I hit the "Find More Sources" option, and, as a precaution, shouted again, and it reconnected... for one minute or so, then to repeat the same thing: thus rode I the rollercoaster through download hell, and was I sorry I'd gotten on, and yet I dared not leap off.

Haunted days, then weeks, ensued. The download would stop and I would desperately order it to resume. Sometimes it agreed, more often it wouldn't. At times the source would disappear for a day or so, but would reappear just in time to revive my waning hopes. I began to imagine, at the keyboard of that host computer on the other side of the world, a pre-conversion Scrooge, a miserable copyright attorney who took cruel delight in waiting for me to connect just so he could, cackling, cut me off. The percentage of download crept up excruciatingly from day to day, again just enough to string me along, keep me from putting the whole sorry business behind me. The internet, too, toyed with me mercilessly, sometimes reaching the speed of 3 kilobytes per second, and dangling before me an etc of just barely by Christmas, before infuriatingly slipping below 1 kps again.

The mushroom of necessity in my febrile brain grew to the point where gnomes hollowed out its stem and installed a little door and windows.

I would leave the computer on throughout the night. I've known smokers whose addictions were so desperate and demanding, they woke up in the middle of the night needing to smoke; I began to awaken in the middle of the night, needing to check on the download.

Alastair brought home a picture he'd drawn in school of a wild-eyed, wild-haired man with his hands in the air, with the caption: "This is my Daddy." In a speech balloon, Daddy was saying "Don't touch the computer!!!!" I looked at the picture. I tried to find its Resume Download option.

One morning, I found that the download had stopped, and no source was available, and, most horribly, the download was gone, my pathetic, hard-won 31 percent was nowhere to be found, had completely disappeared. I straightened up with all the manly dignity I could muster, and said simply, stoically, "So the file-sharing site is in on it, too." I believe that is a reasonably accurate recounting of my words and manner. By extraordinary coincidence, our security guards rushed up to our flat in concerned enquiry just then; perhaps this was as a regular drill, although they seemed to be in the grip of some collective delusion.

Their confusion was strangely exhausting to me, and I took to my bed. It seems I failed to notice that Beauty was trying to make it at the time. I vaguely recall her backing away, mewing in some sort of entreaty, and then racing off.

The bed proved to be unfulfilling, so I sought out Ratan in his quarters.

"Have we anything in the way of a sledgehammer?" I asked him.

"No, sir, sorry," he said with that intolerably irritating politeness of his.

"No? Any sort of anvil, then?"

"No, sir."

"Honestly, Ratan, how are we to maintain a proper household without the basic tools?"

"Yes, sir. Excuse me, sir, why you want?"

"My computer requires repair."

The next days passed in a haze. I performed my professional duties by rote. For the sake of the family, I enacted various undertakings of Christmas preparation. I alone understood what a hollow exercise it would all prove to be, ultimately.

I couldn't look upon the computer with anything but remorse and recrimination. And still, like a lorelei it sang to me of sweet possibilities.

After several days, and just a few days before Christmas, its song and my own curiosity got the better of me, and I searched the faithless file-sharing site once more.

There it was again: "Scrooge 1951".

As with the sudden reappearance of a former lover, my heart jumped, but I feigned the air of a man having moved on, found new, better successes, no longer susceptible to the old charms.

With a nonchalant flick of a casual finger, I clicked the title, and the download began.

Everyone will have his own idea of what qualifies as a Christmas miracle, but what happened in the course of this new download is, in my mind, more than enough to leave the average Readers' Digest subscriber hushed in awe as he reaches for the renewal form: the incessant power blackouts became cessant for its duration, the download began and it never stopped; it chugged along at 5 or 6 kps; when I arose the next morning, it was still at it, and had, by some arithmetical impossibility, achieved over 30 percent.

I puzzled out whatever variables I could imagine, and came up with a scene of the copyright attorney at the other end of the line having slipped and fallen and, weighted by his hideously bloated pockets, unable to get up, but able to follow with impotent rage the percentage of completion reported on his scum-coated computer screen.

Two days later, I watched with breathless, mind-swimming apprehension as the percentage count read 97, 98, 99... and then there it was, 100%. I clicked play, and in a little black box on my screen there appeared the anonymous left hand tracing along the book shelf.

I drifted toward Christmas on a cloud.

On Christmas Eve, I was giddy with excitement, anticipating the thrill of surprise and delight that was so soon to pulse through my dear family. Shortly after we'd choked down our Christmas Eve desert of Ratan's mincemeat pie (he just couldn't get over the 'meat' part of the name, it seemed, and in his own inspired variation on the recipe, seemed to have included a preponderance of hashed goat) as an act of both charity and forgiveness, and after the family arose and reformed in the living room, I meaningfully cleared my throat.

Apparently, it was so Tanyss could speak.

She said, "Grace, sweetheart, why don't you just press play on the DVD player?"

Grace, with a quizzical look, did just that.

The familiar, portentous "buh-puh-bum-puh-bum-pub-puh-bum", flooded the living room, to cries of incredulity, mine loudest among them. (Tanyss later explained that she had, months earlier, emailed her aunt

226

in Toronto with a request that she purchase a copy of Scrooge and mail it to us. We'd always been warned that any mail of any possible resale value would be intercepted and sold before it reached us, so that option hadn't been even entertained by me. Tanyss, however, had instructed her aunt to disguise the disc as something personal and boring, which she'd done. She'd marked it in handwriting as "Pictures of Alastair's party", and indeed it was. Tanyss had received it in delivery to her office with mere days to spare.) We sent gazes of worshipping wonder upon the materfamilias who had somehow wrought this marvel.

But something was terribly wrong. On the television screen, the left hand was a sickly grey-pink, the sleeve an unpleasant grey-yellow, the leather-bound books a muddy rainbow.

"Oh, no!" cried Azien, the movie buff. "It's been colourized!"

The effect on us all, Tanyss included, was similar to what I might expect were I to present a golden roasted turkey and announce "And it's stuffed with a whole marmot."

There was a moment of stunned silence.

"Oh well," Grace said gamely.

"Oh well," the others echoed.

"Ahem," I said, reaching into my jacket pocket for the little paper envelope, "Grace, sweetheart, why don't you just...."

The Tragedy of the Featherweight Turkey, or the fleecin' for the season: Distracted though I was by my descent into download hell throughout the approach of Christmas, other, lesser considerations such as eating would occasionally impose themselves, and as the festive day neared, the unexpected, instinctive hunter-provider I discovered inside myself when I became a husband and father began to kick up a fuss about the prospect of a proper Christmas dinner. Ratan, I concede, is a more adept hunter-provider than I under normal circumstances here, and it's usual for me not to interfere in any way with his management of our home, a happy, rare situation where due respect and undue irresponsibility have no quarrel, but this was a matter where the expertise was all mine. A trip to the market --- not the genuine local public market, which, chaotic, colourful and, um, sensorially-stimulating as it was, held no potential for this objective --- but the exclusive semi-supermarket established to exploit the small international community in Dhaka, the diplomats and aid plutocrats, with a flawed imitation of a "modern western" store stocked with flawed imitations of western brands proved to be dispiriting.

It's typical for the international people here to arrive at this store by chauffeur-driven SUV and to be ushered through the gathered, pressing beggars by baton-swinging guards. My family walks to the store, and when the beggars see us coming, they run up the street to greet us like long-lost kin, very sweet and strange, given that they are all students at our schools, or the children of our students, and see us for hours on a daily basis. I enjoy these encounters, of course, only partly because the sight of me carelessly draped in beggars always leaves the guards visibly confused about what is expected of them, itchy hands twitching on their sticks, so I was pretty cheerful as I entered the store in search of suitable holiday fare. I wasn't really hoping for a turkey, of course, although that would have been no problem in a city such as Bangkok or Singapore, but I'd thought some approximation of turkey might be possible, so I headed to the back of the store where the display counters were, from where, also, the store's stinks radiated.

What I found there approximated turkey in the way a slug approximates a sausage: on display were three tiny, skinned pigeons reddening in the air, and various parts of some goats, which the store labelled 'mutton', most notably several goat heads, skinned but replete with little horns and staring oval accusatory eyes. Dhaka was in the grip of one of its occasional encircling embargoes by the opposition political parties, and the supply of fresh food was suffering, obviously. As always, I considered possibilities arising from what was available to us, and I recollected the little-known "Boar's Head Carol" equally little-known mediaevalists like to sing at the Saturnalia's Feast of Fools. I tried to anticipate the reaction of innocent Alastair and refined Grace as I swung into the dining room holding high overhead in overstated celebration a tray of baked goat heads, belting out an appropriately-amended carol:

> Welcome, welcome, new-born king,
> Welcome, welcome all to our fine festivities,
> Hail ye head of good goatling,
> And remember, the eyes are considered delicacies!

I quickly recognized that would result in a Feast of Fool alone. I turned my attention to the pigeons. One could have stuffed them all with what Alastair leaves on his plate from a sandwich and one sage leaf, and I simply couldn't get past the prejudice that any Dhaka pigeon is necessarily steeped in disease as it, presumably, only gets to eat what the very aggressive and generally indiscriminate house crows have refused, and I didn't care to imagine what that might be. Of course, a family of six dividing three miniscule pigeons....how many germs

229

could there even be room for in half a.... but, still, a 50-50 chance of surviving Christmas dinner was a severely compromised hope.

A desultory inspection of the canned goods revealed nothing any better, and it was in a state of dejection and defeat I departed the store.

Our hopes were elevated somewhat a few days later when a British colleague of Tanyss' told her that the British High Commission had brought in a number of turkeys for its nationals in Dhaka, and that perhaps he might be able to acquire one for our family. Knowing this to be an event quite beyond the imagination or effort of our laissez-faire etc etc Canadian High Commission, Tanyss encouraged him to try his best. And we found out within a few more days that his best was good enough: he reported that a turkey had been reserved for us. Gushing with gratitude, Tanyss still thought to ask how big a bird it was. They were all a good size, he said. He would be delivering it to us by Dec. 22nd. Even for a good-sized turkey, the cost was an emphatic eyebrow-raiser, but what the heck, we thought.

Such was our tender feeling for our benevolent intermediary, Tanyss and Grace set about to prepare him a big batch of shortbread cookies, and they were very good, especially considering that the sugar here is odd, the flour is yet odder, and the butter is so odd we often forget what it's supposed to be. The ingredients are disproportionately costly, here, too, but what the heck, we thought.

I decided that he should have a nice Christmas card to go along with the shortbread, so Gabriel and I went along to the little Hallmark shop, which measures about ten feet by ten feet and has four solicitous young men on hand to assist the shopper in ways we haven't ever deduced. With two young men apiece hovering at

230

our elbows, Gabriel and I pored through the cards on the racks, and this being a wonderful world, we actually found a Christmas card amongst all the vivid Eid Mubarak cards... at least, I think it was a Christmas card: on its front, it indeed said 'Snowings to Xmas' and had a picture of a blue balloon and something that might have depicted a firework or a mutant dandelion; inside, though, it stated "Ritual hands the Splendid, Fineness ever body of", or words to that ineffect. I passed it to Gabriel for his assessment. A young man also read it over Gabriel's shoulder, and nodded his sincere approval.

Gabriel said, "Well, it certainly has greater clarity of message than my birthday card."

"I agree," I said. "But does it properly impart both greetings of the season and our gratitude?"

"Perhaps in its more subtle nuances," Gabriel suggested.

"Quite. But is our benefactor sensitive to subtle nuances?"

"Without knowing that---," he said, shaking his head. The young men were crestfallen.

We went to a folk-craft shop instead, and bought a little card that had an embroidered design in green, red and gold threads. It was nonrepresentational, but the colours hinted at Christmas. It was rather expensive, really, but what the heck, we thought.

We augmented the package with a DVD of a popular movie that had just been released to the theatres in the western world, and it was a good DVD, too, if one could ignore the coughing and moving heads of the cinema-goers, and with a nice bottle of Wilches' Grepe Nictar, and Azien delivered the whole package to our benefactor even before we received the turkey, such was the warmth of our feeling.

Ratan took delivery of the turkey while we were away one day. On our return, he excitedly ushered us into the kitchen to look at it.

It was the first turkey he'd ever seen.

It was the worst turkey we'd ever seen. One of those store pigeons might have bullied it into cringing cower.

"What the heck?" I said, or words to that effect.

"Sir, something is wrong?" Ratan asked.

"A turkey shouldn't nestle comfortably in the palm of one's hand," I said. "One shouldn't be able both to thaw and roast a turkey within an hour."

Ratan regarded the turkey anew.

"Is small turkey?"

"Small turkey? I've pulled bigger giblets out of a small turkey."

"Talk about the slaughter of the innocents," Gabriel observed. "Herod the poulterer. They should have at least given it the chance to hatch."

"Maybe it's a Rock Cornish turkey," Grace offered mirthlessly.

"I'm not even sure this is a turkey," I said. "What do Britons know about turkeys, anyway?"

"Aren't they the ones who hunt wrens at Christmas?" Azien asked. "You don't suppose...."

"It is bigger than a wren," I allowed. "I suspect it's a starling."

Both little Alastair and Ratan looked stricken. Tanyss widened her eyes significantly.

"And by that you mean...," she said.

"And by that I mean it's darling," I said, swallowing my bitter disappointment, which had the useful effect of much diminishing my appetite for turkey. "With the application of necessary care, we'll be feasting on turkey Christmas night." But certainly not thereafter, I thought.

As Wahid pedalled us home after our visit to Sanna Claus at the American Club, I explained to Alastair that, while his wish to Santa had been a good one, it would be hard, if not impossible, to fulfill.

"Santa is very much recognized as being specifically a Christian saint. If all the poor children here were to receive something from Santa on Christmas Eve, some people would object to it as an attempt to convert Islamic children to Christianity."

"That isn't how it should be," he said.

"Yes, well, as you know, we encounter what shouldn't ever be every waking moment here."

The benefit of having a really bright son ---- come to think of it, it's only one of the benefits ---- is that he is very quick to understand, and to allow his reason to inform his desires.

Some things that may be understood shouldn't be accepted, and Alastair's Christmas wish stayed with him, and my pointing out that we were already fully occupied with the difficult efforts necessary to make things better for the children in the long term and permanently didn't satisfy me, let alone him.

"Ratan's daughter is Christian," Tanyss said. "Santa could come to Ratan's daughter on his way to you."

"Yes, that's true," said Alastair.

"You should write a letter to Santa right away, telling him how to find Ratan's village."

"Yes, I will," said Alastair.

Just to be sure, however, on Christmas Eve, after silently forgiving him for the mincemeat pie, I took Ratan aside and gave him a stocking packed full with things a little Bangladeshi girl would like, and instructed him in Santa's traditional methods of secret delivery. It might have been his unflagging politeness, but he seemed excited and eager about the peculiar project.

Then I got to say to him "You'll be wanting the whole day tomorrow, I suppose.", which is always fun for me, if confusing for him.

My family was transported through the miracle of the two Scrooge discs.

Then I called on my three sons to accomplish our next delivery.

In continuing discussion of his wish, Alastair and I had reasoned that surely no one could take exception to a small-scale gesture that was in no overt way attributed to anything about Christmas; so he and I had spent hours in the chaotic jumble that is the public market, selecting from the teeming warren of stalls and tiny shops items for two baby girls and their mother, jerseys and jumpers, toothpaste and toothbrushes, hair brushes, biscuits, little rainbow plastic slinkies, fruit, rice, Nic-Nac chocolates, knick-knack wind-up toys, juice, hand lotion, anything that struck us as suitable.

One big unmarked paper bag to each son, we went downstairs and across to where our footpath family lay sleeping, sleeping without visions of sugarplums, sleeping as though it were just any other night.

I lifted the end of their thin cotton cover, and my three wise sons, bearing gifts from the west to these little stars in the east, placed a bag at the feet of each. I covered the bags, and we four stood back a moment in the smog and bugs swirling beneath the yellow streetlight, heard the breathing of the precious babus and the mother who took up residence on the sidewalk of this neighbourhood because they were too good for the slums, and who squandered half of all her money on a rickshaw ride just to prove it to anyone who cared to look, who railed in utterly mad rejection of all those unseen things

234

that had arranged the difficulties and deprivations of their lives, and I realized that I agreed with her absolutely.

And I looked at my sons looking at them, and I thought "It's beginning to look a lot like Christmas."

I told our student-teachers that Christmas is unlike any other festival in the world. I said that it originated not in a stable in the middle east, but much earlier much farther north, that only in the cold, dark north would it have been so emphatically necessary, and that Jesus' birth was affixed to it after its fact because the meaning of the festival and the meaning of Jesus were so similar: a defiant refusal to accept that apparent death is death, a defiant insistence that life will persist and renew itself despite all the constantly accumulating threats against it. I said that, as man developed, Christmas evolved so that it is now a human festival that might be religious if one wishes, it can work well in a religious context, but is not necessarily so; that this is the gift of the magic: of life, of beauty and health reborn in the midst of dissolution and depravity, of humanity taking an annual moment to imagine itself as its best, an annual moment for us to behave as though we are, to believe, truly, that we are, good.

ASPS (Amarok Society Post Script)

A friend of ours, flying into Dhaka, brought us a copy of the Vancouver Sun. In its pages, we read about how Canada and the world were opening their hearts and wallets, and sending large sums of money to the wealthiest nation in history because one of its cities was experiencing the sort of flood that afflicts Bangladesh annually. I guess people who had a lot of material possessions to lose suffer more than people who never had anything in the first place.

On another page was a grouping of photographs around a column about a gala dinner for some charity. The pictures were of beautiful invitees with their arms around each other, smiling brightly for the camera. I don't mind people having fun at parties, but I couldn't help but estimate that the cost of one those shimmering evening dresses might have kept one of our schools going for a year.

Meanwhile, in local news, immediately local, police discovered a bomb factory next door to one of our schools. They discovered it in a most dangerous way: something in the house started burning. Grace, Gabriel and I were in the school when the fire started. The seeming close call prompted some of our students to dark conjecture, to declare that they would be willing to die for us, personally, and for Amarok Society Women's Schools.

When we first started working with the acutely poor women of our first school, we were teachers and they were beggars; now they're teachers and we're beggars. It's a funny world.

I feel that being a beggar doesn't much suit me, but I don't feel it much suits anyone else, either.

When I travel back to Vancouver and I see 'Help Wanted' signs in all the shop windows along Davie and Denman and able-bodied young people begging on the sidewalks in front of them, my heart doesn't necessarily go out to those beggars; but I've really liked most of the beggars I've known, and many I love, so I can abide that their straits have also made a beggar of me.

The person I most admire in the world is a beggar: my darling Tanyss, PhD, which I now say stands for Panhandler Divine.

By my nature, I'm much more inclined toward the Robin Hood method of fundraising, but Tanyss moderates me with the patient reminder that our procedures must be effective, that the fun part of fundraising is very light, and the preponderant draising part actually has no association with hairraising or cainraising. So I take cap in hand, just as she does, and we go begging.

We were amused (in a way) by the response of one very large agency when we applied for any sort of assistance in dealing with an emergency in one of our slums; a clay oven had been knocked over in a passageway, and before the monsoon put the fire out, more than two hundred houses had been destroyed. As the shacks had been constructed on bamboo poles over a swamp, the displaced people didn't even have a patch of ground on which to crouch in the continuing downpour. The agency answered our appeal with the information that it was impossible for any charity to get into such slums, impossible to gain the trust or cooperation of the people, or manage the corrupt police, the slumlords. We quite enjoy doing the impossible; it makes doing the possible seem so much easier.

Some of the funding foundations we approach appear primarily intent on using their money to verify a world view or further a system of which they approve;

cases in point are the agencies that require our proof that our schools offer a profitable return on investment, that, for instance, the increase in a woman's income after our instruction is greater than the amount we paid to provide it. Munni or Morium would be ashamed to ask such a question, would consider it irredeemably crass, primitive and backward, the political idea that the human experience really can be reducible to monetary quantification.

Tanyss tries to comply, though. I torment her by suggesting she affix a dollar value on the children of our slums not growing up ignorant and frustrated and hopeless enough to be enlisted to carry the bombs. It seems to me that just one person alone not blowing the new Canadian High Commission to smithereens should put us at a clear profit for the rest of our lives, and we've already got thousands and thousands of them.

Here's one for them, though:

Suma was one of our second wave of mothers, those who'd hung back at first, waiting to see how things developed with our pioneer mothers. She was desperately poor; her young husband eked out a few taka as an occasional rickshaw driver, but could find no other income. Suma had two children, a precious little toddler daughter she dressed in a torn dress she'd found somewhere, and a sweet baby girl who wasn't usually dressed in anything; Suma herself was always very poorly attired in the same faded and worn saree. She was very thin, and her life was very hard, but still she was of a cheerful manner and active participation in our school. She was, typically, utterly illiterate when she began. She progressed quickly.

When the price of rice nearly doubled within a short period of time, Suma's family went from undernourished to starving. In desperation, Suma went to apply for work at a garment manufacturer.

The man in the office took one look at this shabby little woman, looking just like all the others who were useless to him, and spoke to her with dismissive sarcasm. "Can you write your name?" he demanded.

"Yes," Suma said.

"Nonsense," he said.

"I can show you," she said, so he gave her a pencil and paper.

She wrote her name readily.

He raised his eyebrows. "Do you know numbers?"

"I know Bangla and English numbers."

"English numbers?" That was of great interest to him.

"What's more," Suma said, "I can read Bangla and English fluently."

"Now I know you're lying," he snorted.

"I'll read anything to you."

He held up a sweatshirt of his company's creation.

"Okay, let's see you read the message on this, if you can read English."

"Ottawa Red Wings, World Ice Hockey League Champions," she read aloud, without any of the confused hesitation I would have shown.

The man was stunned, and not by the ludicrous message. "How can this possibly be?"

"I'm a student of an Amarok Society Women's School," she said.

The usual wage for the women working there is about ten dollars per 72 hour week. Suma was hired at about $13.50 per week, because of the extra value the employer places on her new literacy skills.

240

The problem is, we don't see this as a success story. We didn't teach Suma so she could exhaust her children's key developmental years away in some slave-wage sweatshop. Our hearts' desire is to be able to afford to pay all our mothers a little something that will keep their skills in their neighbourhoods, applied to the neighbourhood children, assuming humanity's responsibility there. That's the way to genuine improvement. That would never satisfy those funding foundations, though, as we won't know for fifteen or twenty years what financial benefit that will have for our real targets, the children of the slums.

So I fantasize about cheerfully diverting Brinks trucks, pressing an invitation upon the guards to join us within our stronghold for one of Rohima's great meals before we send them, considerably unburdened, on their way again.

At any rate, our activities seem less consistent with the legend of Robin and his Merry Band than with the legend of Heracles and his twelve labours, two of them in particular; no one's going to mistake Dhaka for Robin's Greenwood, or scraps of goat for feasts of venison, but those filthy stables Heracles had to clean, or battling the regenerating snake heads of the hydra... those have a real metaphoric familiarity.

We tell our students that they should avoid all opportunities to die for us or for Amarok Society. We tell them that nobler than dying gloriously for the good cause is living humbly for it.

Their good cause is elemental and squarely before them:
to live, learn, teach, love, hope
to fulfil what life requires of them, against all odds.

You are invited to read another amusing story, *The Girl in the Picture*, an endearing tale of the little girl on the cover of this book. If you wish to receive this free story, send an email to us at amaroksociety.org@gmail.com.

Amarok Society, www.AmarokSociety.org, a registered Canadian charity, provides education to some of the poorest children in the world through the power of mothers.

The Munros recognized the need for a sustainable approach to bring education to extremely poor children in these neglected slums – and the great resource that are the mothers in these slums.

Amarok Society teaches extremely poor, uneducated mothers to become neighbourhood teachers, with each mother teaching five or more children.

We invite you to **Adopt a Mother** or make a donation in any amount to make a lasting difference in the lives of the poorest families. Visit www.AmarokSociety.org to the 'donate' menu to find out more.